An Exuberant Catalogue
of Dreams

An Exuberant Catalogue of Dreams

The Americans Who Revived the Country House in Britain

CLIVE ASLET

First published in Great Britain
2013 by Aurum Press Ltd
74-77 White Lion Street, London N1 9PF
www.aurumpress.co.uk

A catalogue record for this book is available from the
British Library.

ISBN: 978 1 78131 094 6

10 9 8 7 6 5 4 3 2 1

2017 2016 2015 2014 2013

Design by Ashley Western
Map design by timpeters.co.uk

Printed in China

FRONT ENDPAPER The south front of Blenheim Palace,
Oxfordshire. The American heiress Consuelo Vanderbilt
married the 9th Duke of Marlborough.

REAR ENDPAPER The Great Hall of J. Paul Getty's Sutton
Place, Surrey. George Romney's portrait of the Gower
family hangs on the left.

PAGE 2 Henry 'Chips' Channon at 5 Belgrave Square, London.

PAGE 3 Consuelo Vanderbilt, as Duchess of Marlborough,
dressed for the Coronation of Edward VII in 1902.

'Damme, they all seem millionaires in America'

the Earl of Emsworth in P. G. Wodehouse's *Something Fresh* (1915)

SUTHERLAND

SCOTLAND

ROXBURGHSHIRE

WALES

GLOUCESTERSHIRE

GLAMORGAN

BERKSHIRE

HAMPSHIRE

DORSET

ENGLAND

LEICESTERSHIRE

NORTHAMPTONSHIRE

BUCKINGHAMSHIRE

OXFORDSHIRE

HERTFORDSHIRE

ESSEX

SURREY

KENT

SUSSEX

BRITISH
Houses Transformed by
AMERICAN
Taste and Money

1. Easton Neston
2. Brook Street
3. North Mymms Park
4. Cliveden
5. Hever Castle
6. West Dean Park
7. Blenheim Palace
8. Crowhurst Place
9. Skibo Castle
10. Floors Castle
11. Moundsmere
12. Hidcote Manor
13. Nevill Holt
14. Hengistbury Head
15. Kelmarsh Hall
16. Ditchley Park
17. Haseley Court
18. St Donat's
19. Leeds Castle
20. Fort Belvedere
21. Belgrave Square
22. Kelvedon Hall
23. Sutton Place
24. Wormsley

CONTENTS

INTRODUCTION

'We are all Americans now,' remarked Sir William Harcourt in 1898, after the marriage of his son Lewis, or 'Loulou', to Mary Ethel Burns, J. Pierpont Morgan's niece.[1] As Gladstone's Chancellor of the Exchequer, who introduced the death duties on landed estates that would undo so many noble families in the twentieth century, he might have been considered to have played a prominent part in setting the scene for the arrival in Britain of so many rich Americans, whose fortunes helped to prop up the declining aristocracy. 'We are the Dollar Princesses', proclaimed one Edwardian song. Harcourt's own case reveals greater nuance than that. He had himself married an American, but not a plutocratically rich one: she was Elizabeth Cabot Ives, the widow of an American naval officer and the daughter of the historian John Lothrop Motley, who became Loulou's stepmother. As for Loulou's American bride, she had spent most of her life in Britain, since her father ran the European end of the Pierpont Morgan bank until his death in 1897; Mary's brother, Walter S. M. Burns, went to Eton and Trinity College, Cambridge. But as Harcourt's quip suggests, Americans – not all of them brides: there were Anglophile men as well – were appearing on the British scene in numbers sufficient to make it a phenomenon.

At the most obvious level, the money infusion kept some country houses going in greater comfort, as well as better decorated, than could have been managed by their hereditary owners. The transatlantic presence also helped to shape the culture of the period. Castles, many of them dilapidated, uncomfortable and uneconomical to run, were bought and revived by Americans. What became known as the 'country house look' was codified by an American. The greatest of early twentieth-century gardens was created by an American. The first female Member of Parliament was an American. It was an American romance that caused Edward VIII to abdicate. It was even an American who enabled that most English of institutions, Lord's Cricket Ground, to build the Mound Stand.

This book examines a selection of country houses (and some town houses) that were supported and sometimes transformed by fortunes hailing from the United States. The earliest example is that of Easton Neston in Northamptonshire, whose owner, the soldier Sir Thomas George Fermor-Hesketh, sailed into San Francisco Bay on his yacht the *Lancashire Witch*, fishing for pretty girls with 'heaps of the needful' and landing Florence Emily Sharon, the daughter of the enormously rich, if notorious, Senator Sharon. That was in 1880, after a painful few years in Britain for the owners of landed estates, thanks to the poor harvests of the late 1870s. Sir Thomas's financial calculation, in looking for another source of 'the needful' than agricultural rents, was an astute one. Farming, hit by foreign imports, would remain in the doldrums until Britain's inability to feed itself during the Second World War was made so manifest to the government that it began a frantic efficiency campaign in the 1950s. Ducal and other very large estates could sometimes find other sources of income on their land, particularly if some of it lay on the edge of an expanding town or city, but owners who could rely only on the traditional mainstay of tenanted farms felt the pinch. They were unable to sell land that had been entailed, a system devised to prevent extravagant children from squandering

What became known as the 'country house look' was codified by an American. The greatest of early twentieth-century gardens was created by an American. The first female Member of Parliament was an American. It was an American romance that caused Edward VIII to abdicate.

OPPOSITE Lord and Lady Curzon outside Kedleston Hall, Derbyshire, shortly after their marriage in 1895. Lord Curzon became Viceroy of India, a marquess and, with the help of his wife's money, a passionate restorer of castles. He adored his wife, Mary Leiter of Chicago, although she found his frequent absences hard to bear.

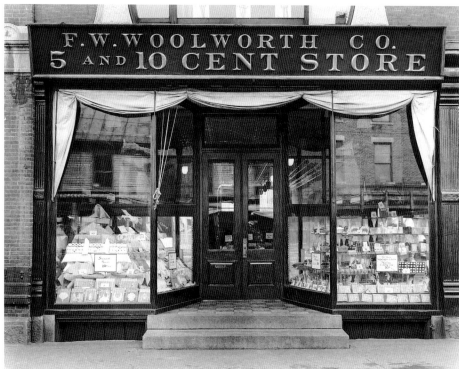

ABOVE The power of the press: the Hearst Building, Chicago, architect James C. Green, 1911. It housed William Randolph Hearst's two Chicago newspapers, the *Chicago Herald and Examiner*, a morning tabloid, and the evening *Chicago American*. Having taken control of the *San Francisco Examiner* from his father in 1887, Hearst became the nation's largest newspaper proprietor. The proceeds allowed him to buy St Donat's Castle in Wales.

LEFT Woolworth's store in early twentieth-century America: offering cheap goods to a newly consumerist public, Frank Winfield Woolworth knew what ordinary Americans wanted to buy. His fortune enabled his granddaughter Barbara Hutton to build Winfield House in Regent's Park, London.

their inheritance, whereby a grandfather would settle the family estates on his grandson, so that the son would only have an interest in them during his lifetime, with access to income but not capital. Such young men were not culturally accustomed to the idea of business: their early manhood was spent in the army, not the City of London, or in a factory or steelworks. At the same time, they were made to feel even more strapped for cash, thanks to the enormous wealth that was now starting to be generated in other parts of the economy and to which they did not have access.

Such young men were not culturally accustomed to the idea of business: their early manhood was spent in the army, not the City of London, or in a factory or steelworks.

Spectacular fortunes were being made from gold, diamonds, finance, retail, oil, shipping and armaments. The new rich would not have found a warm welcome at Queen Victoria's court, but they thronged around the Prince of Wales, whose set included the Jewish financier Sir Ernest Cassell and the grocer Sir Thomas Lipton. Glossy, morocco leather-upholstered motor cars, which often knocked down the animals wandering in the sleepy village streets as their occupants, wearing goggles, veils and floor-length 'dusters', harried the slow-moving round of the old homogeneous country society out of existence, epitomised the change. Toad of Toad Hall, 'a landed proprietor' in Kenneth Grahame's *The Wind in the Willows* of 1909, was not the only one who found the new mode of travel seductive but difficult to afford. Selling the Gainsborough portraits to the art dealer Duveen, who passed them on to collectors such as Frick, might help plug a hole (literally, if the roof was leaking), but did not offer a long-term solution. The game, in some quarters, was transparent. 'ENGLAND'S POOREST DUKE AFTER OUR RICHEST HEIRESS' trumpeted the American press when that impecunious libertine the 9th Duke of Manchester made a play for May Goelet.[2] (Miss Goelet was not impressed. She married the Duke of Roxburghe instead.)

Conditions in the United States were different. Expansion and industrialisation after the Civil War had created wealth, for those who could seize it, on an unprecedented scale. Brides came from families made rich by railroads, finance, shipping, retail, real estate, soap manufacturing, tobacco – all of which contributed to the dowries that were

RIGHT One of US Steel's works in Pennsylvania. Steel made Andrew Carnegie, son of an impoverished Dunfermline hand-weaver, one of the richest men in the world. When he returned to Scotland, from which his family had emigrated when he was a boy, he built Skibo Castle, Dornoch, on an epic scale.

ABOVE There were country houses in the United States, too. Alva Vanderbilt's Beacon Towers, at Sands Point, on Long Island's North Shore, bought by William Randolph Hearst for his wife in 1927. No fewer than sixteen complete rooms from Britain were installed.

so welcome on the other side of the Atlantic. By 1914, 17 per cent of the peerage had American connections.[3] Of course, other countries had their own aristocracies and, in some cases, grander titles – American girls also married men from France, Italy and the rest of Europe – but the British, superficially at least, had more in common with them, and not only the language. By the early twentieth century, rich American families had established their own equivalent of country house life, most visibly on Long Island where hundreds of Gatsby-esque dwellings were constructed, but also around Boston's North Shore, Philadelphia's Main Line and Chicago's Lake Forest and Lake Geneva. George W. Vanderbilt's Biltmore in North Carolina was exceptional in its location and the size of the estate that surrounded it, but representative of an aspiration. As that man of taste Barr Ferree observed in *American Estates and Gardens* (1904):

> The great country house as it is now understood is a new type of dwelling, a sumptuous house, built at large expense, often palatial in its dimensions, furnished in the richest manner and placed on an estate, perhaps large enough to admit of independent farming operations, and in most cases with a garden which is an integral part of the architectural scheme.[4]

Whatever the architectural style of such a house – and eclecticism wandered where it would – commentators recognised that the fundamental concept was British, although with American features such as better sports facilities, a den into which the master of the house could retreat with his stuffed animals and cigars (American social life was run by women) and sound plumbing. It did not win universal admiration – some writers

thought it was un-American – but the urbane art historian Fiske Kimball, setting out to define 'The Country House in America' in 1919, by which time the differences were as apparent as the similarities, noted that 'the traditional country house of England ... has been described as "the perfection of human society"'.[5] The life of the country gentleman represented, for some Anglophiles, an ideal. Thus Colonel Astor of Ferncliff at Rhinebeck, New York, 'approaches the English squire as nearly as such a thing is possible in the Republic that he loves', according to a publication of 1905.[6] The taste endured into the 1930s. When the magazine *Country Life in America* featured Marshall Field III as the first in a series entitled 'Full-length Portrait of a Country Gentleman' in 1934, it announced: 'The Marshall Field conception of a country gentleman is English, and the Marshall Field accent is English.' (Not surprising, since he had been brought up in England and educated at Eton and Cambridge.) His Long Island estate of Caumsett, comprising 2,000 acres of Lloyd's Point near Oyster Bay, typified what might be called the English country gentleman style. Several of his relations were already living in England, enjoying the real thing, among them Nancy Lancaster's first husband, Ronald Tree.[7]

For that enjoyment to be complete, their British homes had to be properly equipped. Americans had higher expectations of comfort than traditional families on the other side of the Atlantic. The latter had been brought up in chilly houses with few bathrooms. The boys were toughened at public schools famous for their rigour. Plumbed hot water seemed, to some people, an extravagance. Far from considering it an indulgence, they preferred servants to carry the water to zinc baths in their rooms. However stately the corridor, ladies' maids had to battle, on behalf of their mistresses, for occupation of a bathroom on it. Americans saw no reason to preserve such a dismal status quo. By the

ABOVE George Washington Vanderbilt's Biltmore House in North Carolina, designed by Richard Morris Hunt in the French Renaissance style and built 1888–1895. Frederick Law Olmsted laid out the estate with forests and a new village.

The Marshall Field Garden Apartments (architect Andrew J. Thomas), the construction of which was subsidized by Marshall Field III to provide low-cost housing in Chicago, Illinois, 1933.

LEFT Marshall Field III, heir to a department store fortune. Educated at Eton and Cambridge, he was thought to typify the Anglo-American gentleman by *Country Life in America*.

time Sir Edwin Lutyens was building Middleton Park, in Oxfordshire, in the 1930s, the second Lady Jersey, the film star Virginia Cherrill, ex-wife of Cary Grant, could demand fourteen bathrooms, her own (because the bathroom was now regarded as a design project in its own right) being onyx. Americans also expected warmth, hence a dowry was often used to install central heating. Few seem to have been attracted to the Arts and Crafts movement, with its note of primitive austerity. The exception was the actress Mary Anderson at Broadway, in the Cotswolds, a village that had first been discovered by American artists and writers. Henry James was appalled by Court Farm, Mary Anderson's home: 'You, if I may say so, have made yourselves martyrs to the picturesque,' he wrote after a visit. 'You will freeze, you will suffer from damp. I pity you, my dears.' He would not have had the same worry at Moundsmere, the large English Renaissance-style house that Sir Reginald Blomfield designed for Wilfred Buckley. Mrs Buckley had specified that the bedrooms should be arranged as suites: a pair of sleeping chambers would be separated by a bathroom and – another American innovation – closets.

To people with means, crossing the Atlantic was not – except for the unfortunate passengers on SS *Titanic* – as perilous as it had been in Charles Dickens's day. When he first crossed to the United States on the Cunard Line's *Britannia* in 1842, his state room was an 'utterly impracticable, thoroughly hopeless, and profoundly preposterous box', in which he was seasick and fearful during heavy seas. The decline of landed incomes during the 1870s coincided with the appearance of larger and better ships. Wooden hulls and paddlewheels had been replaced by iron hulls and screw propulsion. By the Edwardian age, shipping lines were vying to outdo each other in the luxury that they offered, and many country house owners, used only to taking houses, when necessary, or staying with friends, rather than in hotels, must have first encountered the convenience of compactly planned suites with adjacent bathrooms when crossing.

> Mrs Buckley had specified that the bedrooms should be arranged as suites: a pair of sleeping chambers would be separated by a bathroom and – another American innovation – closets.

Europe had become accessible to Americans with means, and travel books such as Mark Twain's *Innocents Abroad* and novels such as James's *The Portrait of a Lady* explored how their countrymen reacted to the leisurely tours that could be made. For their part, Europeans were equally struck by their visitors, particularly the type known as 'the American girl'. She was almost unreservedly a good thing. She was likely to be better educated than her equivalent in Europe, where it seemed hardly worth spending money on educating female offspring because their future in life would be assured through marriage; it was thought – wrongly, as the popularity of the American girl would prove – that men were put off by signs of cleverness. On the contrary, it was considered delightful that the American girl could converse on a wide range of subjects. Nancy Astor exemplified, in heightened form, another characteristic of the American girl. She was thought to be livelier than any product of a British upbringing, having, in some cases, been allowed a greater degree of independence; the prospect of a misalliance was not so formidable in the United States as in the caste-bound aristocracy of Europe. Fault was not constantly being found with her, in terms of her failure to live up to inherited standards, or what the aristocratic code had laid down. On the contrary, explained Henry James in *The American Scene*:

> She had been grown in an air in which a hundred of the 'European' complications and dangers didn't exist, and in which also she had had to take upon herself a certain training for freedom ... she could develop her audacity on the basis of her security, just as she could develop her 'powers' in a medium from which criticism was consistently absent. Thus she arrived, full-blown, on the general scene, the least criticized object, in proportion to her importance, that had ever adorned it.

'The American girl' became a legend. 'I may say that the two factors in American life which have always made the profoundest impression upon me,' observes Mr Faucitt in P. G. Wodehouse's *The Adventures of Sally* of 1921, 'have been the lavishness of American hospitality and the charm of the American girl.'[8]

If the American girl offered a devastating combination of money, liveliness and quite possibly looks, the appeal of the British male had been assumed to rest in his title.

Lord and Lady Curzon in India with the Nizam of Hyderabad, while Lord Curzon was Viceroy. Curzon deeply mourned his wife Mary Leiter's death in 1906. In 1917, he married, less happily, another American, Grace Hinds, a rich widow from Alabama.

Around sixty American women became peeresses, but of these many could not have been certain that their husbands would get the title. In some cases, it depended on a freak sequence of events that could not have been foreseen. The 9th Baron Strabogli married Elizabeth Cooper of Sacramento in 1884; but it was not until thirty-two years later that he succeeded in claiming his peerage, which had been in abeyance for several centuries. Other inheritances followed equally tortuous routes. May Goelet evidently knew her worth on the market and would settle for nothing less than a coronet. She had, though, been Consuelo Vanderbilt's bridesmaid at her wedding to the Duke of Marlborough and so knew the ropes. Other girls must have been happy to marry into aristocratic families and take a chance, knowing that the odds were against them. British men were regarded as chivalrous; they could seem to be the living representatives of a long history; and London, for all its smoke and fog, was still the centre of the richest empire ever known. 'There is only one place and one great society in the world and that is London and the English,' declared the Hon. Mrs Michael Herbert, May Goelet's aunt Belle, in 1893.

Crossing the Atlantic gave some women the chance to reinvent themselves. Maud, or Emerald, Cunard, who we shall meet later in this book as the chatelaine of Nevill Holt in Leicestershire, began life in San Francisco. The west coast of America was, at the end of the nineteenth century, still far enough from New York for her past not to worry her there, and it was forgotten altogether by the time she had married an English baronet. In time, Lady Cunard divorced her heavy-set, fox-hunting husband: part of the character of the American girl was that she moved on, and divorce did not hold for her quite the terror that it did for her British sisters.

Equally, men did not always marry for money – some fell for actresses and chorus girls. When the dreadful 8th Duke of Manchester, then Lord Mandeville, married Consuelo Yznaga in New York in 1876, she and her mother having supposedly nursed him back to health after he had contracted an African fever, she was not specially wealthy; the large fortune that she acquired later probably came from her successful brother. As this example shows, social contact between the United States and Britain had increased: not only did American families come to Europe but European families travelled in the US. Some failed Etonians became cowboys. Urban Huttleston Rogers Broughton's father did well from mining, railways and digging sewers in the US, and married an heiress to boot; their son was educated at Harrow, created Baron Fairhaven (after his mother's home town) and bought Anglesey Abbey in Cambridgeshire with his brother Henry, near their

ABOVE Mr and Mrs Robert Tritton bought Godmersham, Kent, once the home of Jane Austen's brother Edward Knight, in a destitute condition in 1935, and employed Ogden Codman, Edith Wharton's associate, to remodel it. Elsie Tritton had previously been the wife of Sir Louis Baron who made a fortune from Black Cat cigarettes. Regularity was given to the façades; panelling and architectural features were salvaged from the great London houses then being demolished for redevelopment.

Newmarket stud. The gardens made by Lord Fairhaven at Anglesey Abbey are now owned by the National Trust.

ABOVE LEFT Rococo stucco in the new orangery at Godmersham Park, decorated by Felix Harbord.

ABOVE RIGHT Bedroom hung with landscape wallpaper of the architectural monuments of Paris.

Cosmopolitan though some were, Americans were not always prepared for what they found in their new homes. We have only Consuelo Vanderbilt's polished memories of her marriage to Sunny, since the Duke's private papers, if they exist, are still locked up in the Blenheim archive, but her account of her reception at Blenheim has the ring of truth. The nineteen-year-old bride, transported to a land far from family and home, was thrown into a milieu in which everyone else – mostly older people – knew the rules, but not her. Protocol was a minefield. She had to master dozens of strange names, with complicated forms of address; she had to run a household of several dozen servants, where the butler would not stoop to put a log on the fire when requested, but offered to call the footman to do it. She entered a world that was frosty, emotionally stunted, poorly travelled, philistine and rude. Her husband, the misnamed Sunny, saw his role as being only that of a 'link in the chain', one generation of Marlboroughs passing its heritage to the next, life possibly enhanced. The British Empire was at its zenith, and the family was walled up within an impenetrable belief in its cultural superiority. Consuelo would not have been surprised by the conversation that old Lord Scarsdale had with his daughter-in-law Mary Leiter from Chicago, who had recently married his son George, the future Viceroy of India and Marquess of Curzon:

'Last night at dinner he said, "Do you have sea fish in America"; "I suppose you don't know how to make mince pies in America"; "I suppose you don't know how to serve a good tea in America. We only know how to do it in England."'

Families who preserved their position through dynastic or mercenary marriages accepted that both parties would find love in unions not blessed by the Church, and smart country house parties were constructed to allow adulteries to take place. It was not a recipe for marital success. Sir Thomas George Fermor-Hesketh found that his wife preferred a more stimulating society than that of Northamptonshire, where he spent his leisure hours in a workshop making motor cars. Mary Burns did not draw a good card in Loulou Harcourt, despite his climb through the political ranks which saw him raised to the peerage as Viscount Harcourt. 'He is simply a sex maniac,' complained Dorothy Brett, daughter of Lord Esher, whom he assaulted. It was 'so tiresome' that he was 'such an old roué. He is as bad with boys as with girls ... It isn't that he is in love. It is just ungovernable Sex desire for both sexes.'[9] But Lord Curzon, whom contemporaries found

RIGHT Anglesey Abbey, between Cambridge and Newmarket, bought by Huttleston Roger Broughton, Lord Fairhaven, with his brother Henry in 1926. Lord Fairhaven was remembered by the gardener Graham Stuart Thomas as spending 'most of his time pursuing beauty in many different ways', particularly by the planting of thousands of trees. Avenues, for which he had a passion, often terminated in urns or sculpture. Another romantic house to attract Americans was Ightham Mote in Kent. In the late nineteenth century Ightham Mote became home to Queen Palmer, wife of General W. J. Palmer, the railroad engineer who founded Colorado Springs. In the 1920s, a young American called Charles Henry Robinson came to see it. He fell so deeply in love with it that, chancing to see it advertised in 1953, he bought it on impulse. He restored the house and being, like Lord Fairhaven, without wife or children, gave it to the National Trust in 1985. Anglesey Abbey had been left to the National Trust on Lord Fairhaven's death in 1966.

unendurably arrogant, adored Mary Leiter and, on her death in 1906, built a memorial to her in the form of a chapel attached to the church at Kedleston. He would later say that he was not afraid of death because he would meet Mary in heaven; his tomb effigy lies next to hers – an arrangement that could not have been tactful to his second wife, Grace, the Alabama-born widow of Alfred Hubert Duggan of Buenos Aires, whom he married in 1917.[10] Not every transatlantic alliance ended in tears.

The supply of heiresses dried up around 1910. In 1914, the world of slow-moving, finely tuned, well-heeled continuity that the country house represented was blown apart by the First World War. Throughout the war, the losses from the officer cadre were higher than those of other ranks. Many heirs to country houses were among the dead; many country house families found themselves prematurely struggling with the death duties that Harcourt had introduced. Shortly before the First World War, a number of aristocrats, offended by Lloyd George's People's Budget and the weakening of the House of Lords, had begun, where they could, to sell estates. After 1918, the trickle of sales became a flood. A quarter of England is said to have changed hands.

Before the United States joined the Allies in 1917, Americans in Britain had been energetic in organising hospitals and raising funds. They had also been active during the Boer War of 1899-1901, when Minnie Paget, the daughter of American hotelier Paran Stevens, staged a Masque of Peace and War, at which her own costume from Worth, of black crêpe de chine decorated with gold scarabs, was reputed to cost $6,000. The American Ladies Hospital Ship Society equipped the hospital ship *Maine*. But the Anglo-American effort had been more muted then, Britain's role as the imperial power apparently bullying the Boer farmers being more difficult to sell to the descendants of the War of Independence. Britain's cause during the First World War could be represented as morally right. Anglo-Americans were keen to demonstrate their allegiance, even though their native country was undecided. The conflict had different consequences for the two nations. Far fewer of its soldiers were killed than those of the European armies (less then 10 per cent of those of France, about 13 per cent of those of Great Britain – despite having a much larger population). The searing effect of loss in Europe can be compared with that of the Civil War in the United States, except that the American Civil War was followed

by decades of buoyantly self-confident growth, whereas in Europe the story was one of uncertainty, disillusion and stagnation. After 1918, the American trajectory continued upwards, while Britain – particularly the Britain of the old landowning elite – faltered. Before the war, families like the Marlboroughs may have unquestioningly assumed that they were conferring a favour on anyone who married into them. After it, glamour passed to the United States. These were the Hollywood years. The irascible, stamp-collecting King Emperor George V stuck to the assumptions of the Edwardian age, including the belief in the innate superiority of British ways. His son the Prince of Wales could see that America was modern; he wanted part of it.

Between the wars, Americans living in Britain could lead society in a way that had not happened in the Edwardian period. In London, Maud Cunard created one of the few salons, along French lines, where artists, writers, politicians and princes were to be found in the same room; perhaps it took an American's lack of social inhibition to achieve it. Her rival Laura Corrigan – a one-time waitress from Chicago who married a doctor, then fell in love (while still married) with a Cleveland playboy whose father owned a steel company – began a social assault on London after James Corrigan's death in 1928, using her immense wealth to buy going-away presents of such value that few people could resist her soirées. Two of the most prominent political sets of the period – at Cliveden and Leeds Castle – were presided over by Americans. Meanwhile, Nancy Astor's niece, Nancy Lancaster, née Perkins of Virginia, was becoming the acknowledged queen of taste in the decoration of country houses. Perhaps it took an American eye, trained in the traditions of the Southern states, to see that a simpler way of life did not have to mean a less elegant one. Mrs Robert Tritton's divorce settlement from the man who manufactured Black Cat cigarettes enabled her decorator husband to remodel Godmersham Park – a house in which Jane Austen used to stay – as an exquisite example of the Georgian Revival, using the American architect Ogden Codman, co-author, with Edith Wharton, of *The Decoration of Houses* (1897).

What effect did Britain have on the heiresses and millionaires who came to it? The men were often susceptible to the romance of history: it was European culture that had attracted them in the first place. William Waldorf Astor's tastes were definite and in some ways eccentric, but he adored Cliveden and Hever Castle, treated their architecture well, filled them with rich and intriguing things, and drew on his years in Italy to create gardens. He adopted British nationality during the First World War and became a member of the House of Lords. Walter Burns's North Mymms Park became a more cosmopolitan version of the Frick Collection in New York. When in Scotland, Andrew Carnegie, in blaring tweeds, became almost a caricature of a Scottish laird – his castle, Skibo, so big that he and his wife had to go somewhere else to feel at home. It must have given Carnegie, whose family had left Dunfermline in poverty, a thrill to beat the British at their own game. He was one of the few Americans to build a completely new country house. Most of his compatriots focused their creative energies on old properties, modernising them, making them comfortable but also intensifying the romance or the period elegance. Owners took up the cause of their adopted country, particularly during the First and Second World Wars; they rode to hounds, hosted cricket matches, entered public life, sent their sons to Eton and, in the case of 'Chips' Channon, became more English than the English.

The Americans found British country houses at a low ebb. Not only were family pictures being sold abroad, but decorators could also supply entire rooms, either to museums or to private owners, acquired from houses that were demolished or had been neglected. William Randolph Hearst gobbled up many such salvages, from Britain, Italy, France and Spain, for the mega-ranch of San Simeon in California; others were installed at St Donat's Castle, the property in Wales that he visited no more than half a dozen times. As John Harris has shown in *Moving Rooms*, the taste was nothing new. When the Duke of Chandos's great house of Cannon was dismembered in 1747, every scrap that could be removed was seized upon by architects, masons and sculptors. Today the process would be called recycling, and praised. But the volume of old fireplaces, panelling and

Perhaps it took an American eye, trained in the traditions of the Southern states, to see that a simpler way of life did not have to mean a less elegant one.

ABOVE Alexander Forbes-Leith, dressed for yachting. He became the 1st Baron Leith of Fyvie in 1905. His only son Percy predeceased him, dying while serving in the Second Boer War. Percy is remembered by a full-length window by Louis Comfort Tiffany in Fyvie church.

plasterwork – Godmersham Park was almost wholly remade with them – reflects the rate of demolition, particularly of Georgian London but also the country house. To take just one example from the United States, the Boston Museum of Fine Arts received rooms from Hamilton Palace, Lanarkshire, in 1924; Newlands House, Gloucestershire, in 1937; Woodcote Park, Surrey, in 1928; Kirtlington Park, Oxford, in 1931; and Croome Court, in Worcestershire, 1951. By definition, these were all interiors of museum quality. The Americans in Britain propped up houses that the traditional owners could not afford to maintain. The Duke of Sutherland, whose family had outshone the royal family in the nineteenth century, was glad enough to get Sutton Place off his hands, even at the modest price that he received from J. Paul Getty.

Applying his fine discrimination in matters both of business and connoisseurship, Getty filled Sutton Place with richness, in the form of paintings, tapestries, antiquities and gold plate. These acquisitions were not destined to stay with the house but eventually found their way to the Getty Museum in California. It was left to Getty's son, knighted as Sir Paul Getty, to provide British galleries and museums with fighting funds with which to do battle in the auction room. We not only have one of the loveliest cricket pitches in England to remember him by, but Canova's *The Three Graces*, now in the Victoria and Albert Museum.

The Americans did more than bring money to the beleaguered British country house: they supplied hope and inspiration. To appreciate their contribution, we need look no further than the castles that they restored.

ABOVE Kimbolton Castle. Viscount Mandeville, future 8th Duke of Manchester, married Consuelo Yznaga, whose father came from a Cuban family, in 1876. Her fortune was not enough to prevent him from being declared bankrupt in 1890. A friend of Edith Wharton, Consuelo was one of the models for her unfinished novel *The Buccaneers*.

Hever Castle was a lowly farmhouse until purchased by William Waldorf Astor; Leeds Castle, in the 1920s, had become a project that only a woman of strong will, backed by Whitney money, could take on. William Randolph Hearst could not be called the saviour of St Donat's since it had been put into good repair by his predecessors, but Martin Conway, art historian and mountaineer, could not have rescued Allington Castle in Kent without the backing of his wife, Katrina, only child of Charles Lambard (who built the Chesapeake and Ohio Railway) and stepdaughter of Manton Marble, former owner of the New York World. Saltwood Castle in Kent was picturesque but gloomy and ultimately unaffordable to the Deedes family in the 1920s; it only looked up after being purchased by Reginald Lawson, a great-grandson of one of the printers of the *Daily Telegraph*; his reclusive American wife Iva took a detailed interest in its restoration after Lawson shot himself in 1930. (She later married the widowed Martin Conway.)

Tattersall Castle in Lincolnshire was due to be dismantled and shipped to the United States; the National Trust rejected the proposal to acquire it, having not elicited a sufficiently strong response from a public appeal. It was Lord Curzon, whose financial security owed everything to two American marriages, who saved it, along, in due course, with Bodiam Castle in Sussex and Montacute House in Somerset, all three properties being passed to the National Trust.

If an Englishman's home is his castle, it might be because he married an American.

FLORA SHARON

AT

EASTON NESTON

I n 1876, at the age of twenty-seven, Sir Thomas George Fermor-Hesketh became the 7th Baronet of Rufford. Inheriting from his brother, Sir Thomas, the 6th Baronet, who died young, he had already established a career as a soldier. Eton was followed by Sandhurst. In the shabby colonial adventure of the Zulu War of 1879 he served Sir Redvers Buller, VC, as a 'galloper,' and fought at the Battle of Ulundi, when the Zulu capital was taken. Before leaving for the war, he judged that he had 'sufficient of the needful' to commission an elegant, three-masted steam yacht, the *Lancashire Witch*, and in 1880 he took some friends on a world cruise.

PREVIOUS PAGES Easton Neston, Northamptonshire, built for Sir William Fermor (later Lord Lempster) around 1690 and soon remodelled by Hawksmoor. In 1880, Sir Thomas George Fermor-Hesketh was one of the first country house owners to marry an American heiress.

Florence or Flora Lady Fermor-Hesketh, née Sharon, painted by the Belgian artist Emile Wauters in 1895. Flora married Sir Thomas George Fermor-Hesketh in 1880.

The first leg of it was spent shooting and sightseeing, but when the craft approached San Francisco, the seafarers sharpened their game. They were aware that they stood a good chance of meeting pretty American girls with plenty of the needful. The story has it that Sir Thomas George had been able to rescue some citizens of San Francisco from a watery grave off the coast of Mexico and so his name preceded him into the city. This earned him something of a hero's welcome, which he was happy to exploit. One of his companions described their time in port:

Nothing could exceed the Kindness and Hospitality of everyone we met. Head gave us a dinner party – had some very pretty girls to meet us. We spent a most enjoyable evening, never left the house til 2.30. I met a Miss Crocker, a very nice girl with heaps of the needful. Francis got hooked on and has landed her I think. Hesketh has two on hand, both very nice ... Can't make up his mind ... I must say American girls are very pretty, dress well, have good feet, lots of fun and very sharp. Some have lots of money.'

ABOVE LEFT Senator William Sharon, 1821–1885, made rich by the Bank of California and the Komstock Lode: even by the standards of the West, he lived scandalously, but gave his daughter Flora a dowry of $2 million.

ABOVE RIGHT Sir Thomas George Fermor-Hesketh, 7th Baronet, (1849–1924) in a portrait hanging at the Hesketh seat of Rufford Old Hall, Lancashire: a country gentleman in search of 'the needful'.

LEFT The *Lancashire Witch*, on which Sir Thomas George Fermor-Hesketh and a party of friends set out on a round-the-world cruise in 1880, shooting animals and looking for American wives.

When Sir Thomas did make up his mind, it was not in the direction expected: 'To my astonishment Hesketh has been making love to Miss Sharon, a most charming girl, daughter of Senator Sharon. The engagement was announced in the *Chronicle* and Newsletter … We used to spend some very jolly times together from Saturday to Monday at Belmont, Senator Sharon's country seat. Everything was done to perfection there.' Photographs show that Florence Emily Sharon, known as Flora, had the good looks of her compatriots – although her strong jawline also suggested determination of character. The dowry of $2 million that she brought with her was the biggest yet to come from the United States and would not be exceeded until Consuelo Vanderbilt married the Duke of Marlborough fifteen years later. It lifted the curtain on a golden era for marriages between American heiresses and British aristocrats, which lasted thirty years.

Two worlds had come willingly into collision. Sir Thomas George Fermor-Hesketh of the Rifle Brigade, an honorary colonel of the Liverpool Regiment of Militia, was, in his tastes and outlook, a characteristic product of the Victorian ruling caste, who would bring back not only an American bride on the *Lancashire Witch* but also a variety of dead animals that he had shot; after the taxidermist had stuffed them, they would decorate the couple's country seat.

William Sharon, born in Ohio, was equally an American type. Small of stature, with dainty hands, he nevertheless joined the California Gold Rush of 1848 when in his twenties. Having worked for some years in real estate, he went to report on the state of the Comstock Lode that had recently been found in Nevada. He found that exploitation of the great silver deposits was at a standstill. The mills had too little capital; the small banks had lent at high rates of interest but could get neither the interest paid nor capital returned; miners could not be paid; the greatest activity on hand was provided by lawsuits. Sharon went into business with William Ralston of the Bank of California and reorganised the operation, building a railroad to transport the ore and directing production. He became the King of the Comstock.

When crisis struck in 1875, Ralston was found dead in San Francisco Bay, possibly from suicide. Sharon, however, kept his nerve. He succeeded in reviving the bank, a stupendous achievement for someone with little experience of banking, in a young,

RIGHT Boudoir at Easton Neston, showing a sumptuous juxtaposition of mellow tapestries and very smart French furniture. The boat-shaped Empire bed, with bronze-gilt mounts, is a *lit en bateau* of around 1800, made in Paris.

ABOVE Two views of Ralston Hall, 22 miles outside San Francisco, which William Sharon renamed Belmont, was originally built for his business partner William Ralston of the Bank of California. Belmont was one of the 'most magnificently hospitable mansions in California'. Two thousand invitations were issued for a party to meet former president Ulysses S. Grant. For Flora and Sir Thomas George's wedding reception the Metropolitan Orchestra was brought from New York.

frontier community. The day before Ralston died, he had signed over the deeds to his entire business empire to Sharon, the subsequent reorganisation of which Sharon kept well out of public view (quite a lot simply vanished, to the disappointment of creditors). He became owner of the newly built Palace Hotel (the expense of which had been one of the causes of the financial collapse), as well as the celebrated country house Belmont, which Ralston had built 22 miles from San Francisco.

By saving the Bank of California, Sharon had saved many businesses and depositors from ruin. Sharon was too hard-boiled a character to attract plaudits. His business dealings were conducted on the same amoral principles as his private life. He bought the favours of women as cynically as he manipulated the price of silver. Even cosmopolitan and buccaneering San Francisco thought it a bit much.[2] Although lent dignity by the title of Senator, his record of attendance was one of the worst in the history of the Senate; he is recorded as having been seated at only five sessions. Instead of the legislature, he preferred his rooms – and assignations – in the Palace Hotel, San Francisco, and at Belmont.

With typical business thoroughness, he investigated Sir Thomas's background. 'Hesketh is a good one,' he puffed to cronies, through what had become a shapeless straggle of moustache. 'I doubted him at first, and sent three men to Liverpool and London – it cost me $10,000 – to hunt up his record. It was a good one. But I say [to Senator Jones] it would have been a jolly idea if Hesketh had concluded at the same time to hunt up mine, eh?' Sir Thomas may have concluded that he knew all that was necessary. There was no doubting Sharon's wealth, and the bride and groom would be living a long way from California.

Belmont was regarded as being among the three 'most magnificently hospitable mansions in California'.[3] Ralston had spent lavishly on stables and paintings; he was a bull market man. An arcade of ionic columns surrounded the parlour; gilded chairs with tapestry seats stood on the floral carpet. Two thousand invitations were issued for the fête given for Ulysses S. Grant, embarking on a world tour after an inglorious presidency. The wedding reception given for Flora and Sir Thomas was equally convivial. Guests were regaled with music by the Metropolitan Orchestra, brought over especially from New York. But California, which would learn to take flamboyant entertaining in its stride during Hollywood's heyday, was not as yet used to such rich fare, and it was too much for some tastes: a cartoon in Ambrose Bierce's *The Wasp* portrayed it as a revel of drunken hogs.[4]

The house to which Sir Thomas took Flora, on the other side of the Atlantic, was Easton Neston, in the prime fox-hunting county of Northamptonshire. While Sir

They at once began to buy gold lacquer glove boxes, a lacquered ostrich egg, 'some lovely cabinets', two 'very handsome vases and a very old bronze pot for $3,000'.

LEFT The dining room at Easton Neston. It may have been that William Kent had a hand in this room, but the stuccadore probably worked without supervision, since the swirling stucco picture frames sometimes sit awkwardly with the architecture. The elephant by the fireplace was probably brought back from Sir Thomas Fermor-Hesketh's travels in the *Lancashire Witch*.

Thomas was away, it had been let. One of the tenants in the mid-1870s had been the Empress of Austria, still remembered for the dash she cut with the Pytchley. (Frederick Sandys's portrait of Sir Thomas at Rufford Old Hall, in Lancashire, now owned by the National Trust – the Heskeths came from Rufford – shows him in a hunting coat, crop in hand, against an old tapestry of a hunting scene, as though to make the point that he was continuing a centuries-old tradition of the chase.) Although Belmont had been comfortable and well appointed, East Neston was – as Sharon had called its owner – 'a thoroughbred'. The giant Corinthian order of the entrance front 'endows the house with ... unparalleled nobility', according to Sir Nikolaus Pevsner in the Northamptonshire volume of *The Buildings of England*. It is built of stone – 'the finest building stone I have seen in England', as John Morton described it, in *The Natural History of Northamptonshire* of 1712. The architect was Nicholas Hawksmoor, perhaps with some involvement from Sir Christopher Wren. It was built in the years around 1700 for the connoisseur Sir William Fermor, who was raised to the peerage as Baron Leominster in 1692 and purchased some of the Arundel Marbles that are now in the Ashmolean Museum, Oxford. Above the nine-bay façade is emblazoned the Fermor motto – *Hora e sempre*, 'Now and forever'.

But California, which would learn to take flamboyant entertaining in its stride during Hollywood's heyday, was not as yet used to such rich fare, and it was too much for some tastes: a cartoon in Ambrose Bierce's *The Wasp* portrayed it as a revel of drunken hogs.

AO SAL MDCCII

ABOVE The east front of Easton Neston, designed by Hawksmoor in 1702. The grandeur of Ancient Rome is evoked through the pioneering use of the giant order. This photograph from 1927 shows the topiary and parterres of the garden complemented by statuary.

The *Lancashire Witch* now disgorged the treasures (and animal skins) that she had brought back from her travels. They included a discriminating collection of oriental art, some purchased during a stop in Japan. After Commodore Perry steamed into Tokyo Bay in the 1850s and Japan became open to the West, a craze for Japanese fans, textiles, prints and bibelots swept the more artistically inclined drawing rooms of Europe. The taste could still be satirised in Gilbert and Sullivan's *The Mikado* (1885) and exalted in Puccini's *Madama Butterfly* (1904).

Sir Thomas's party arrived at Nagasaki, having looked in on Singapore and Bangkok, in January 1880. They were not only surprised to find men and women bathing naked together, but entranced by the works of art they saw in the temples. They at once began to buy gold lacquer glove boxes, a lacquered ostrich egg, 'some lovely cabinets', two 'very handsome vases and a very old bronze pot for $3,000'. On 3 February, 'our curio man brought on board a wonderful collection ... [Sir Thomas] bought some lovely things.'[5] Sir Thomas entered into the spirit of the country: a photograph shows him, thinning hair immaculately parted in the centre of his head, the points of his moustache neatly groomed, in Japanese dress – presumably made for him specially, down to the wooden pattens on his feet, since he would have been taller than the average Japanese.

Oriental objects found their way into every room at both Easton Neston and the family's house at Rufford (where the Georgian rectangularity of Rufford New Hall had superseded the extravagantly carved Ruffold Old Hall for family occupation in

RIGHT The formal garden and lake at Easton Neston, kept in immaculate condition until its sale in 2005, thanks to a succession of American marriages. It is now owned by the Russian-born American Leon Max.

ABOVE Sir Thomas Fermor-Hesketh, 1st Baron Hesketh (1881–1944): son of Sir Thomas George and Flora Fermor-Hesketh. A soldier and Conservative MP, he was raised to the peerage in 1935.

RIGHT The present Lord Hesketh and his brothers Robert and Johnny enjoy Easton Neston in the 1950s.

the eighteenth century). Tall blue and white pots were complemented by gorgeous cloisonné dogs, cockerels and incense burners, as well as delicate *objets de luxe*, such as a tortoiseshell box in the form of a fish. Architecturally, they were fortunate in their choice of J. A. Gotch to tailor Easton Neston to the needs of late Victorian life: a local man, he was also an architectural historian who published several books.

Two sons were born in quick succession. After the marriage, Flora and Sir Thomas drifted apart, she disappearing increasingly to London, which she found more cheerful than the shires, and he into a workshop where he developed an early motor car.[6] The older of the boys, Sir Thomas, 8th Baronet, a politician who was created Baron Hesketh in 1935, inherited his parents' oriental taste, becoming a keen collector of Chinese art. He also followed his father in marrying an American, his step-cousin Florence Louise Breckinridge, in 1909.

They did not follow Lord Beaverbrook's example of adding a cinema to Easton Neston (at Cherkley Court in Surrey, Beaverbrook's was in the Art Deco style of the old Daily Express building in Fleet Street; there he used to watch the same western over and over again – agony for his lieutenants, who found they were the only ones awake once the great man had fallen asleep). Instead, Lord Hesketh furnished the local town of Towcester with a free-standing cinema as a present for Florence, who loved movies. Opened in 1939, it had a private entrance and box; being neurotically afraid of objects falling on her head, Lady Hesketh would sit there beneath an umbrella.

In 2005, the present Lord Hesketh sold Easton Neston and almost everything in it at a country house auction conducted by Sotheby's. Once again, an American came to the rescue of the house. After it had languished, forlornly, on the market for several months, Easton Neston was bought by the Russian-born fashion retailer Leon Max.

ABOVE HM Queen Mary visits Easton Neston in 1937. On the far left is the 1st Baron Hesketh, next to him stands his eldest son, the Hon. Frederick Fermor-Hesketh, who became the second baron, with his brother Hon. John Fermor-Hesketh on the right.

WALTER
BURNS

AT

BROOK STREET &
NORTH MYMMS PARK

I n Victorian London, Walter Hayes Burns represented a new phenomenon in the world of finance: the American banker. There were few enough of them by modern standards, but the great railroad and industrial concerns of the United States needed financing, and offered spectacular returns to Europeans who called the market right. He brought to England a flavour of plutocratic taste in America – cosmopolitan, sumptuous and epic.

PREVIOUS PAGES
The long gallery at North Mymms. Opulent tapestries and heavy Renaissance furniture are combined with Elizabethan plasterwork and dark panelling. The absence of clutter may reflect the demands of the *Country Life* photographer who took this shot in 1934.

Hubert von Herkomer's portraits of Mr and Mrs Walter Hayes Burns of North Mymms, 1895. Walter Burns married Mary Lyman Morgan, daughter of the banker Junius S. Morgan, in 1867.

Although Burns's parents came from New Hampshire and Philadelphia, he was born in Paris. Some of his education took place in France, as a result of which he spoke fluent French; this proved to be of benefit in his business life. He finished his studies at Harvard, before beginning his career as a clerk of a company dealing in dry goods, Morton, Grinnell and Co.; one of the principals seems to have gone into banking and Burns went to London to open a branch of L. P. Morton, Burns and Co. there. In 1867, he married the girl who had been his neighbour on Madison Avenue – an astute move, since she was Mary Lyman Morgan, the daughter of Junius S. Morgan. The marriage took place in London. Thereafter, business seems to have palled, for a couple of years later he gave it up. He took his wife and family to live in Paris. But he soon got his hand in again, becoming the European director of the US Mortgage Company and Paris manager of the London Banking Association. By 1878, his father-in-law must have thought he had served his apprenticeship, since he made him a partner. His experience of Europe and his fluent French made him the natural candidate to run Morgan's London office.[1]

A portrait of Burns survives in the Cornish country house of Antony, now owned by the National Trust. Painted by Hubert von Herkomer, it shows an uncompromising looking walrus-moustached gentleman, sitting four square to the spectator, shrewdly appraising him through poached-egg eyes. His style is very much that of his brother-in-law, John Pierpont Morgan. The picture dates from 1895, the year of an American financial crisis: J. P. Morgan saved the American government from default with a loan whose terms were criticised as being more than favourable to the banker. From Burns's corpulence and his florid complexion, it comes as no great surprise to learn that he died two years later. Herkomer, who painted in a chiaroscuro style, was not the best choice to paint women, and his companion painting of Mary drapes her in a pall of gloom. Burns seems to have been too much the banker to spare time for frivolities, but he and his wife lived up to the standards expected of international millionaires, in terms of both decoration and art.

In 1884, Burns bought 69 Brook Street in London's Mayfair, a house of 1725; the building firm of C. H. Trollope and Sons was employed to add an extra storey. Six years later, he acquired the neighbouring house (of 1726), number 71, which was almost immediately demolished and rebuilt, to be merged with number 69. Externally, the Grosvenor Estate, which owned the freeholds of the properties, forbade the use of red brick, as Burns had wanted; instead, an unexceptional stone-coloured stucco façade resulted. But the interior, which survives today as the Savile Club, is in a different spirit altogether. Those who enter leave behind the restrained near-uniformity of a Victorian terraced street and enter an opulent series of rooms in the French taste. A Parisian architect, Dutch-born William Bouwens van der Boijen, who specialised in expensive *hôtels particulier*, was brought over for the job. Burns probably knew the Hôtel Cernuschi by the Parc Monceau, built for the banker Henri Cernuschi in 1873–74, if not the Villa Stéphanie at Houlgate, in Normandy, for another banker, Albert Kahn. He felt as comfortable in Paris as London. As Americans, he and his wife would have been attuned to the French styles brought home by American architects who had studied at the Ecole des Beaux-Arts. It was as much the style of the Upper East Side in New York as of Newport, Rhode Island.

By the Edwardian decade, London had also succumbed to the allure of the *dix-huitième*. The elegant neoclassicism of Mewès and Davis's Ritz Hotel on Piccadilly of 1906 seemed the last word in metropolitan

At Brook Street the French note is sounded as soon as the visitor has passed the front door. The entrance hall is square and dark: the French panelling has been stained, rather than painted, creating the rich effect of a millionaire's mansion in New York.

LEFT The staircase at the Savile Club, which now occupies the Burns' house in Brook Street. An opulent look was achieved by the use of French panelling and a rich ironwork balustrade.

chic. In the early 1890s, Mr and Mrs Burns were advanced in their appreciation of French styles, although not alone. Bankers, being an international community, found them particularly seductive. They were the basis of the *goût* Rothschild, made manifest at Waddesdon Manor in Buckinghamshire and other Rothschild country houses. On South Audley Street, the millionaire Dutch banker H. L. Bischoffsheim was translating the interior of Bute House into faultless *dix-huitième* French as the setting for his picture collection. Often, rich clients – and they generally were rich – who wanted French decoration could buy genuine examples of it, in the shape of panelling removed from old houses in Paris, swathes of which had been demolished by Baron Haussmann in his remodelling of the city. But the craftsmen who could make exact copies or produce new boiseries in the same idiom also existed. Sometimes it took an expert to tell reproduction from the real thing, and as the wood aged it became almost impossible to do so.

At Brook Street the French note is sounded as soon as the visitor has passed the front door. The entrance hall is square and dark: the French panelling has been stained, rather than painted, creating the rich effect of a millionaire's mansion in New York. This space contains the main staircase with its handsome ironwork balustrade. A second staircase sweeps up to the ballroom in such a theatrical rococo style that it would serve as an appropriate stage set for *Der Rosenkavalier*. Painted beige, it was heavily gilded, while cupids frisked around the cove of the ceiling. Such frivolity was too much for a London gentleman's club of the 1920s, and the gilding was painted out, the panelling rendered in heavy colours and the cupids banished. (It was charmingly redecorated in about 1980 but without cupids.²)

As soon as their London mansion was finished, the Burnses bought a country house. Their choice fell on North Mymms Park, built around 1600 in a position that had always enjoyed easy access to London, being on the Great North Road, near Hatfield. They employed Ernest George, one of the busiest country house architects of the day, then in partnership with Alfred Yeates, to add a big new wing to the south-west. This was done sympathetically, in a similar style to the Elizabethan original, but, although doubling the floor area, on a scale that keeps the new work subordinate. The centre of the new wing was a loggia, testimony to the country house owner's embryonic desire to bring more sunshine and fresh air into living spaces. This front contained the dining room, a second

ABOVE A fifteenth-century French Madonna in the gallery bay at North Mymms Park. The photographs on these pages were published by *Country Life* in 1932. The atmosphere is that of the period rooms in an American museum.

RIGHT Spectacular but comfortable: the South Hall at North Mymms Park, Hertfordshire. Walter Burns commissioned the prolific country house firm of George and Yeates to double the size of the late Elizabethan mansion. The fireplace on the left is carved with a bas relief by Harry Bates. The music gallery, which crosses the room at first floor level, is concealed by one of many tapestries.

ABOVE Built around 1600, North Mymms Park, Hertfordshire, conveniently near London, was one of the best examples of the late Elizabethan style in England. George and Yeates enlarged it in a sympathetic style, redecorated the interior, erected stables, reorganised the approach, built lodges and a bridge.

entrance hall, offices and (when an extra floor was later added) nurseries. By this date, the Elizabethan and Jacobean styles had become second nature to Ernest George, who, in the words of the *Country Life* articles published in 1934, 'gave free play to his love for the picturesque elements' in them. Craftsmanship was of the highest order, with plaster ceilings modelled by Walter Priestley receiving particular praise.

It may have been that North Mymms was conceived as a retirement project. Alas, Burns did not live to enjoy it long: he died in 1897. By the time it was photographed by *Country Life*, it had become even richer than Burns could have known it, since Mary had inherited part of her brother John Pierpont Morgan's collection. It is shown without Victorian palms or conversationally arranged groups of furniture, but as a succession of carefully composed harmonies of masterpieces. A fifteenth-century French sculpture of the Madonna and Child stands in front of a bay hung with tapestry, lit by an elaborately wrought electrolier. A seventeenth-century bust stands on a richly carved side table, in front of a Mortlake or Soho tapestry of the elements: below the tapestry (in the new entrance hall) the dado is made of richly figured marble. The dining room was designed by Waldo Story, with marble floor and a coffered ceiling in the Italian Renaissance style: a suitable showcase for Italian works of art. Mary having died in 1919, North Mymms was now owned by the Burnses' son, Walter S. M. Burns, who followed his father into banking. British country house owners, who, after the First World War, were struggling to make ends meet — and in many cases were parting with the masterpieces that hung on their walls — must have been astonished by North Mymms, whose ambience strongly recalled that of the period rooms in some of the great American museums.

THE ASTORS

AT

CLIVEDEN

&

HEVER CASTLE

About the time of the American War of Independence, John Jacob Astor left the Old World for the New. Coming from the village of Waldorf, near Heidelberg, Germany, he was the fifth son of a butcher but saw an opening in musical instruments. An extraordinary meeting while travelling to America diverted his course. The brig that he crossed on, the *North Carolina*, became icebound in Chesapeake Bay with a number of other ships; passengers walked from one to another over the ice, and it was in this way that Astor met a young fellow German who traded in furs. Astor became intrigued by the lucrative business and soon entered the fur trade himself. The Iroquois on the Canadian border traded animal skins for cooking pans and pocket knives; Astor's profit was 1,000 per cent.

PREVIOUS PAGES Sir Charles Barry's palatial Cliveden House, Buckinghamshire. As the frieze's Latin inscription, written by Gladstone, proclaims, it was rebuilt for the 2nd Duke of Sutherland.

Nancy Astor wearing the 55.23 carat Sancy diamond in the tiara given to her as a wedding present by her father-in-law, William Waldorf Astor (right).

Surplus cash was invested in farms on the edge of the expanding port of New York, which became some of the most desirable real estate on Manhattan. At the time of his death, Astor was the richest man in America. Later generations invested, less profitably perhaps, in British country houses, which provided the background to their lives and, in one case, a political scandal (widely known as the Profumo Affair) that shook British society to its foundations.

Like other children of the exceptionally rich, John Jacob Astor's great-grandson, William Waldorf Astor, found it difficult to relate to his contemporaries. Born in 1848, he had endured a joyless childhood. Unlike his father, who rarely took a holiday, Astor hated business. He rejected the Calvinism of his upbringing and likened his first exposure to Greek philosophy, with its idealisation of the human body, to the conversion of St Paul. An effort to find a purpose for himself in national politics, as a Republican, was woundingly rebuffed by the notoriously aggressive American press.

The post of United States Minister to Italy, which he accepted in 1882, suited him perfectly, not least because it allowed him to leave his native land for three years. In Rome, his duties were barely perceptible, and he had more than enough time to collect marbles, take lessons in sculpture and start writing historical romances. In 1890, the year

ABOVE Party time in the library at Cliveden: Nancy and Waldorf Astor with five of their six children, with hats, rocking horses and cracker.

LEFT In the foreground is the balustrade from the Villa Borghese in Rome. Beyond it, part of the formal parterre of clipped yew pyramids and wedge-shaped beds edged with box hedging, a simplified version of the bedding introduced in the 1850s.

of his father's death, he left the United States for good, reportedly declaring 'America is not a fit place for a gentleman to live'. Three years later, he bought a country house that was not merely gentlemanly but aristocratic: Cliveden Place, in Buckinghamshire.

Cliveden, on its outcrop overlooking the Thames – the 'cliff' from which it takes its name – is an upright house, rising, in two stages, above a terrace. The garden front was built by Charles Barry, with A. E. Pugin, one of the architects of the Houses of Parliament, for the 2nd Duke of Sutherland in the mid-nineteenth century. It is in the sumptuous Italianate style that he had already deployed for the Duke at Trentham Hall. Little of the earlier house, originally by the gentleman architect and soldier William Wynde, survived Barry's remodelling; but Astor was more than alive to the vivid personalities who had inhabited it.

Cliveden was not a house that had passed down through several generations of the same family, but, being only twenty miles from London and about five from Windsor, had changed hands quite frequently. The potential of the site had been spotted by the notorious libertine and politician George Villiers, the 2nd Duke of Buckingham – whose name stands for the B in CABAL, Charles II's coterie of ministers. John Dryden wrote of him that:

In squandering wealth was his peculiar art:

Nothing went unrewarded but desert.

(Dryden had reason to dislike Buckingham, having been pilloried in his play *The Rehearsal*.) Rather than choosing a sheltered position, Buckingham built for show – and, unusually in an age not yet alert to the charms of picturesque landscape, to take advantage of the glorious views. The diarist John Evelyn, who visited 'that stupendous natural Rock, Wood & Prospect of the Duke of Buckinghams' in 1679, bore witness to the 'extraordinary

Expense' of the building, but admired the result. The house, he wrote,'stands somewhat like Frascati on the platforme is a circular View of the uttmost verge of the Horison, which with the serpenting of the Thames is admirably surprising'.[1]

Buckingham was followed by the Earl of Orkney, a soldier, who employed Thomas Archer to add wings attached by colonnades in the early eighteenth century; and in the 1730s, Orkney's daughter, the 2nd Countess in her own right, leased the house to Frederick Prince of Wales. Astor had bought Cliveden from the 1st Duke of Westminster, another man whose property interests, after the development of Belgravia, had made him very rich indeed.

In London, Astor had already commissioned the jewel-like Astor Estate Office, beside Temple Inn: a sumptuous French Renaissance caprice whose weathervane was in the form of a gilded caravel. Its architect, John Loughborough Pearson, was better known for churches and Truro Cathedral than country houses. Nevertheless, Astor employed him to refashion Cliveden as a setting for his collection of ancient statuary, old furniture, armour, musical instruments and curiosities. The hall was opened up, the staircase redesigned. It was typical of Astor's love of romantic history that the newel posts of the latter should have been carved as idealised figures from Cliveden's past: William and Isabella de Turville, who had owned the estate in the twelfth century, and the Duke of Buckingham and his mistress, Anna Maria, Countess of Shrewsbury.[2] The terrace was adorned with a baroque balustrade which he had bought in Rome. It came from the Villa Borghese.

Astor, a big man with piercing blue eyes, had always been mistrustful and autocratic. These tendencies became exaggerated after the death of his wife Mary at the age of thirty-six, shortly before Christmas 1894. He grew increasingly introspective. The weekend

parties that he threw at Cliveden were significant, as Michael Astor describes in *Tribal Feeling*, for their lack of *joie de vivre*.

> Guests were told exactly when to arrive; and when they arrived they were greeted by a secretary [or by Astor's fourteen-year-old daughter Pauline, on whom the unenviable role of chatelaine had descended] …who showed them to their rooms and told them where, and at what time they would assemble before meals. The rest of the weekend was according to a schedule, short periods set aside for walking, driving, resting, eating, and finally sleep.[3]

Deviations from the schedule – even by guests who wanted to leave – were not permitted. Coming back from the United States in 1905, Astor's elder son, Waldorf, met Nancy Langhorne Shaw, a beautiful, outspoken Virginian divorcee. When they were married the next year, Astor gave them Cliveden, which then opened a new chapter. He retired to Hever Castle in Kent, which he had bought in 1903. Not only a castle, but the childhood home of Anne Boleyn, Hever was better suited to his antiquarian tastes and collection than suave Cliveden. By now, John Loughborough Pearson had died, but his son, Frank Loughborough Pearson, continued the practice. He was given the job of bringing Hever, a relatively small and self-contained antiquity, which had fallen into use as a farmhouse, up to the de luxe standards of an Edwardian country house.

From 'splendid gloom', characteristed by tapestries and 'ancient leather', Cliveden acquired a more feminine note, or as Nancy put it: 'The place looked better when I had put in books and chintz curtains and covers, and flowers.'

Cliveden, on its bluff overlooking the Thames. The house had been owned by the Duke of Sutherland and the Duke of Westminster before William Waldorf Astor bought it in 1893.

In an article in the *Pall Mall Magazine* what was described as 'the daintiest of castles, a castle in miniature, a castle-ette, of the feminine gender' was rescued from its fallen agricultural condition. (The author of the piece was almost certainly Astor himself, whose laboured style is unmistakable; he had bought the magazine to publish his own writing.) The courtyard was virtually reconstructed around the surviving Tudor timbers, Pearson adding gables with elaborately carved bargeboards and dormers. Visitors passed figures in armour, as well as 'many a precious specimen of the artificer's skill and taste', on their way to the inner hall, graced with a fireplace of Verona marble and panelled in walnut. The walls were hung with portraits of Anne Boleyn and Anne of Cleves, the latter having lived at Hever from 1540 to 1557.

Astor's storyteller's imagination delighted in objects that had been owned by figures from history or had witnessed stirring deeds. Thus the richly carved screen of columns dividing the inner hall from the passage were made from a tree cut down in Caserta in 1747, later turned into a wine press. 'Fire and tempest, the lightning's blast it escaped; wars and revolutions left it untouched'; finally it was bought by the timber merchant who sold it to Astor. 'Nor, indeed, does its history end here, for a piece of an ancient rapier was found embedded in its heart, a romantic circumstance which our imaginations may interpret as they will.'

Astor, who had a paranoid streak and kept a large sum of money in ready gold, in case, presumably, of revolution, slept in the castle itself. The drawbridge was restored

and it was pulled up at night, while patrols of smart young policemen, who might have been taken for house guests, combed the grounds. Twenty-five guest rooms, as well as the new kitchen wing, were provided on the other side of the moat. They were built so that the whole looked like a medieval village. The idea was unique to Hever and cannot be found in any other country house. To Astor, though, it seemed entirely natural. His deep passion for old places and artefacts made him sensitive to the castle's integrity; he wanted to equip the castle for his needs as a country gentleman, while protecting it from an addition that might have overpowered it or detracted from its romance.

In order to harmonise with the existing structure, the new work had to take on some of the mellowness of age. So the Home Counties were scoured for old tiles. Stone walls were built as though they had been patched with brick, the upper floors being timber-framed. The neo-vernacular style is similar to that which George Devey had used in the 1850s for estate buildings at Penshurst Place, a few miles away.

In December 1904, 748 workmen were employed on the castle, village and garden, each receiving a Christmas present of two pounds of beef, a slice of cake and threepence worth of tobacco. That was before work had begun on excavating the lake, which in itself employed 800 navvies. One man's job was carrying forty-five gallons of beer to How Green every day for them to drink. There were also eight detectives employed to work in shifts round the clock monitoring the grounds. Astor, whose middle name, some said, should have been 'Walled-Off', knew that secrecy would excite general interest. His work also provoked criticism. Philip Tilden, who restored Allington Castle, said of Hever:

> Hever Castle might indeed have been another Bodiam, infinitely alluring as it sat as I first saw it in the 'nineties, with its grey skirts sweeping the waters of the moat, set around with the blue swords of the wild flag; but instead it has now become a miniature Metropolitan Museum of New York.[4]

But the *Pall Mall Gazette* thought, it seemed that 'only an anchorite' would have lived in an unmodernised castle.

> A moat cannot defend us from a clammy dampness, coating even the inner walls and floor with a mysterious growth where lurks a host of ills which prey on man. So modern wit steps in, and Hever Castle now rests upon a lower floor of asphalte.

Astor may have become a British subject in 1899, as well as a peer in 1916, Viscount Astor of Hever Castle, but he retained American expectations in the matter of comfort. Hever was inherited by Astor's second son, John Jacob Astor V, who became

ABOVE LEFT Unlikely friends: Nancy Astor and George Bernard Shaw, two opinionated expatriates strongly attached to their roots, leaning against the terrace balustrade at Cliveden.

ABOVE RIGHT Queen Elizabeth at Cliveden, in conversation with Margaret Truman (left), daughter of President Truman, and Mrs. Walter Gifford (centre), wife of the United States ambassador to Britain.

OPPOSITE ABOVE Lord and Lady Astor take a train.

OPPOSITE BELOW Nancy Astor, with bouquet, hears her election to the House of Commons proclaimed at Plymouth in 1919. The defeated Labour candidate, William Gay (left), takes it well.

RIGHT This aerial view of Hever Castle in Kent shows the late fourteenth-century castle owned by the Boleyns in the foreground, with Frank Loughborough Pearson's 'medieval village' (which housed a guest wing and services) beyond the moat. As part of his landscaping operations, William Waldorf Astor diverted the river Eden.

ABOVE An old photograph of Hever shows it clad in creepers and with water lilies in the moat. Astor, who was apt to be paranoid, pulled up the drawbridge at night.

RIGHT The King Henry chamber at Hever Castle, photographed in 1907. Henry VIII was supposed to have visited Hever – and even slept there – while pursuing the Boleyn girls, Mary and Anne. Some of his letters are addressed to Anne at Hever.

ABOVE The long gallery at Hever with ceiling by Frank Loughborough Pearson. Hever was in a bad way when Astor bought it in the 1890s. He filled it with old and curious furniture, selected for the romantic associations that it evoked. Note the suit of armour at the end of the room.

1st Baron Astor of Hever Castle. Educated at Eton, he was a first-class athlete, horseman and tennis player, who won Olympic medals for racquets in 1908. He fought bravely in the First World War, losing a leg in 1918. His father left Hever so that he and his family could live there on his return. He, in turn, respected his father's taste and memory by leaving it largely untouched. In business, he developed his father's magazine and newspaper interests (William Waldorf also owned the *Observer*) by buying *The Times*.

Cliveden became famous as a political powerhouse, which gave its name to the 'Cliveden Set', a group of highly educated right-wingers who favoured an accommodation with Nazi Germany over war. In 1919 Waldorf, an MP, severed relations with his father after the latter accepted his peerage, knowing that it would force him to resign from the Commons on William Waldorf's death. Waldorf's loss, however, was Nancy's gain, and she was elected Britain's first female MP.

Hard-working and diligent, Waldorf had a perfect foil in the diminutive, effervescent Nancy – variously described as 'a grasshopper', a 'Chinese cracker' and 'a Gnat'.[5] William Waldorf might have been expected to react against a divorcee, but instead took to her: a present on her coming to Cliveden was a stupendous tiara containing the 55-carat Sancy diamond (now in the Louvre). (Typically, this jewel derived added lustre from its provenance, having been owned by James I and Charles I and worn by Louis XV at his coronation.) Waldorf made it clear that he would never return to Cliveden on leaving it, and Nancy took him at his word. From 'splendid gloom', characterised by tapestries and 'ancient leather', the house acquired a more feminine note, or, as Nancy put it: 'The place looked better when I had put in books and chintz curtains and covers, and flowers.'[6] In the hall, a floor of Minton tiles was replaced by stone flags. Gloomy antiquities were banished. There was considerable anxiety when William Waldorf did make a return visit on the birth of his first grandson. To everyone's relief, he was charmed.

WILLIE JAMES

AT

WEST DEAN PARK

A fixed star in the social firmament of Edwardian England, for the set that orbited around the King, Edward VII, was the race meeting held every August in West Sussex: Glorious Goodwood. Every year but one, the King stayed at Goodwood House itself, entertained by the Duke and Duchess of Richmond. Only once, in 1899, was he able to accept the hospitality of Mr and Mrs Willie James at nearby West Dean. The eighty-year-old Duke had refused to invite, as a French paper put it, two ladies 'à la presence desquelles le prince tenait beaucoup'. The Jameses had no such inhibitions. Afterwards the King pointedly declared that it had been the best Goodwood he could remember. The Duke and Duchess were so mortified that they claimed him back the next year. Still, the story says a lot about the new age and about West Dean. It was just his sort of house. Even the family motto seemed to fit: 'J'aime à jamais' – 'I love for always'.

PREVIOUS PAGES Mr and Mrs Willie James of West Dean Park, Sussex. He inherited a fortune from his American merchant father, she was a baronet's daughter and intimate of Edward VII. It is unlikely that the diminutive and witty Evelyn was really reading: she was too short-sighted.

William Dodge James was the youngest of three brothers. His father, Daniel, had been born in Hartford, Connecticut, in 1801, coming to England in his late twenties as the representative of Phelps, Dodge and Co. By temperament, Daniel was a merchant, importing cotton from the United States and the tinplate of which Wales was then the world's largest producer, used for manufacturing household items from tin baths to tin cans. He fretted over his partner's speculative investments in land, factories and railroads. But he was good at what he did, and his middle son, John Arthur James, continued the business, expanding into just the sort of areas that Daniel himself had wished to keep clear of – vast copper mining interests and railroads – and with equal success.[1]

Willie did not go into business. As a boy he had been sickly and was taken abroad by his brilliant eldest brother, Frank Linsly James. Frank had gone to Cambridge and then studied law, but he never practised the profession. Instead, he devoted his energies to exploration and big-game hunting. Willie, whose health must have recovered, joined him

on many of these expeditions. According to his entry in *Who's Who*, Willie travelled in the Sudan, Abyssinia, Somaliland, Arabia, Afghanistan, the west coast of Africa and the Arctic. He had been a member of the party that made the first European ascent of Mount Tchad-Amba in Abyssinia, beneath a hail of rocks flung by monks from the monastery at the top. He helped map the upper reaches of the Khor Baraka, and spent the winter of 1882–83 exploring the Somali coast in an Arab dhow.

Frank published *Wild Tribes of the Sudan* in 1883 and *The Unknown Horn of Africa* in 1888. He had, in addition, 'literary and artistic tastes', which were manifested in the fine library and superb collection of eighteenth-century proof engravings he formed at the house at 14 Great Stanhope Street, London, where he lived with his two brothers. He was also a discriminating scientific collector and published a work on microscopy.[2] This was quite a sibling to live up to and Willie did not try to compete intellectually. But there was also sport, a passion they could share. The game book for December 1881 to April 1882 records a total of thirty-five beasts, including a lion, two buffalo and ten gazelle. Lions, when they were shot, were stuffed and put in bamboo and glass cases in the entrance hall at West Dean. It all came to an end in 1890, when Frank was killed by a wounded elephant he was attempting to shoot in Gabon. Willie, however, had already decided to settle down, having been married the previous year.

His bride was Evelyn, the eldest daughter of a Scottish baronet, Sir Charles Forbes, and a niece of the Countess of Dudley. They made quite a pair. Willie was the very image of a 'good fellow': steady-eyed, erect, immaculately groomed, his moustaches curled, shown in the portrait by R. Brough (an obscure painter: Willie was not an aesthete) with riding crop in hand. Evelyn was petite, clever and lovely, with the prettiness and *retroussé* nose of an eighteenth-century porcelain figurine. She was also extremely myopic, which forced her to wear spectacles (removing them gave her the faraway look that she has in

ABOVE Mrs Willie James drives a pair of beautifully matched ponies in the grounds of West Dean Park, Sussex. Both female and equine elegance were admired in a house which competed with nearby Goodwood to entertain Edward VII.

OPPOSITE Wrapped up warm: King Edward VII, in layers of tweed, with Mrs Willie James in furs to his right. West Dean was very much the King's sort of house.

ABOVE The entrance hall at West Dean decorated with trophies of Willie James's big game shooting expeditions (note the rug). The cut velvet brocade around the doors is typical of the opulent effects beloved by the Edwardian plutocracy.

RIGHT Billiards was played on a well-lit table, with comfortable settees for those watching.

RIGHT Decoratively, the Edwardian ideal: an eclectic mélange of ultra-comfortable upholstery, potted palms and curiosity (note the sedan chair), organised with maximum opportunity for informal groups and private conversation, and a display of royal photographs in frames. A brave attempt has been made to meet the design challenge of electric light.

contemporary photographs). In an article on 'Beauties of Today', *Vanity Fair* characterised Lady De Grey as magnificent, Lady Helen Vincent ethereal, the Duchess of Devonshire stately and Lady Eden 'Madonna-ish', but Mrs James as unquestionably witty.

The architect Edwin Lutyens, who visited West Dean when he built Monkton, a small house in the woods to provide an escape from West Dean's formality, in 1902, recorded an unflattering first impression: 'Roundabout bar maid,' he wrote to his wife, Lady Emily, 'quizzy, cynical and conceited.' But even he was eventually won over. 'Gay thoughtless extravagant as she has rights to be; beautifully dressed lovely rings: makes all the noises and squeaks that only a little woman may dare make.' She was celebrated for amateur theatricals in which house guests were expected to take part.

Once, when the Jameses were staying with Baron Hirsch in Hungary, she dressed up as a peasant woman begging for alms and apparently fooled the whole party. Going to church, she asked the nanny to get ready one of the children to go with her. 'Which one?' the nanny asked. 'Whichever goes best with my blue dress,' she replied.

They chose West Dean because it was fashionably near Cowes – Willie also inherited

> In an article on 'Beauties of Today', *Vanity Fair* characterised Lady De Grey as magnificent, Lady Helen Vincent ethereal, the Duchess of Devonshire stately and Lady Eden 'Madonna-ish', but Mrs James as unquestionably witty.

Frank's yacht, the *Lancashire Witch*, and became a member of the exclusive Royal Yacht Squadron at Cowes – and Goodwood, and had some of the best shooting in England. The wedding presents give an idea of the style of the house. The Prince and Princess of Wales gave a sapphire and diamond brooch, while other jewellery included diamond necklaces, diamond pendants, diamond brooches, diamond earrings, diamond bracelets, diamond aigrettes, diamond combs, diamond tiaras and diamond crescents, with a sprinkling of other stones. Smaller presents included two silver button-hooks, a gold-mounted walking stick, a silver string-box, an easel (an adjunct of nearly every smart drawing room, and used for displaying pictures rather than painting at), a paper cutter, menu holders, a silver crumb-scraper, two silver moustache brushes and a polar bear. The polar bear, which was stuffed, held a lamp in one paw and a tray for visiting cards in the other, and was put in the entrance hall.

In 1896, while still Princess of Wales, Alexandra actually stayed at West Dean. It was the first time she had spent the night in the house of a commoner, and the magazine *World* hailed the event as a landmark:

The polar bear, which was stuffed, held a lamp in one paw and a tray for visiting cards in the other, and was put in the entrance hall.

Until this surprising 'end of the century' not even a Prince had stayed in any but the most important houses. At one time the visit of a monarch or an heir-apparent made the greatest of great ladies, great statesmen or great courtiers, greater. But by degrees the line has been drawn lower and still lower, until at last of very few rich people it can be said that they have never had Royalty under their roofs … Mrs James fulfils the conditions of her time – she is amusing.

It was a quality that Edward VII desired from the succession of beautiful women – Mrs Paget, Mrs Greville, the Duchess of Marlborough, Lady Londonderry, Mrs Arthur Sassoon, Lady Troubridge, Lady Lonsdale, Mrs Cornwallis-West and, above all, Mrs Keppel – who beguiled his last years.

Mrs James was probably also his mistress – at least that was the talk. Certainly her son Edward looked remarkably like his royal namesake, although he had a different theory: that the King was his grandfather, Mrs James Edward VII's daughter. Either way, he liked staying at West Dean.

The house stood on an 8,000-acre estate which James had bought for £200,000 in 1891. Although long and low, the Wyatt house was in the castle style, faced in knapped flint, with an ecclesiastical window over the porch. The architects who renovated it for the Jameses, Ernest George and Harold Peto, had a very large practice building very large houses. George and Peto substantially altered the south façade – replacing the porch with a *porte-cochère*, building a tower, raising the low link wing to the east, constructing a new service court and adding a wing full of bachelor bedrooms. 'So bad, I think,' moaned Lutyens, when he saw the result. But the major work of remodelling was done inside. An oak hall – 34 by 30½ feet – was created by knocking two existing rooms into one and removing the ceiling, so that it went up through two storeys. Next to it a new staircase was put in with solid oak treads. A billiard room, with the table lit from above, was added next to the smoking room, and the rooms on the south front were redecorated and made to open into each other to form an enfilade, which had advantages for entertaining. Marble replaced stone in the entrance hall, and all the damask and much of the panelling was

LEFT Entrance hall at West Dean. Animal heads on the walls and a polar bear holding a tray for visiting cards.

ABOVE RIGHT Edward James and his wife, the dancer Tilly Losch, his wife from 1930–34. During their marriage, the stair carpet of Monkton House, on the West Dean estate, was woven with her footprints; after their divorce, it was replaced with one bearing the paw prints of James's dog.

RIGHT The tennis court at West Dean was particularly attractive, with its thatched pavilion beneath the cedar tree. The ugly netting is restricted to one side, allowing the court to blend into the landscape – although there must have been lost balls.

RIGHT Edward James, Britain's
greatest patron of the Surrealists,
at home in Wimpole Street, London.
Behind him is Picasso's *Seated
Woman with a Hat*. Composer Igor
Markevitch lounges on the right.

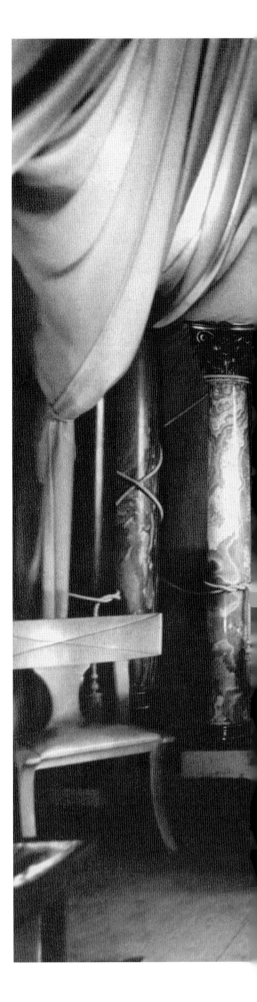

renewed. Old Masters – mostly Flemish and Dutch, with paintings by Cuyp, Rembrandt, Ruysdael and Steen – were bought at London sale rooms to hang on the walls. It must have been the oak hall that prompted the studio to remark, perhaps roguishly, that for West Dean's 'progenitors one has not to turn to old France, nor to Lombardy, but to England, and to "Merrie England" at that'.

The atmosphere at West Dean was in marked contrast to the faded gentility of some more ancient seats, and Edward VII, with his eye for the comforts of life, must have known it. The house was equipped with every form of modern technology. Electric lighting was installed, and there were 364 incandescent bulbs – or 'burners' as they were called – throughout the building, some of them attached to hideous brass lanterns. Pounding away in the engine house behind the stables were two single-cylinder steam engines which gave off up to twenty-one brake horsepower at 170 revolutions per minute. An extra engine and dynamo were kept in readiness in case additional power was required. Strictly speaking, three batteries would have been sufficient to store the necessary current, but the battery house contained five, since – out of consideration for the boiler man – it was decided not to run the engines on Sundays.

It was said that West Dean perfectly fulfilled that desideratum of royal entertaining in the Edwardian age: that servants should magically materialise at your elbow when they were needed and be invisible when they were not. Equally, guests did not see many of the other domestic arrangements, like the hydraulic dinner lift from the kitchen (installed by the American Elevator Company) or the automated steam laundry, one of the first in the country. As a precaution against fire, there was an electric pump capable of discharging 1,500 gallons of water an hour from a reservoir constructed in the hills above West Dean, and hydrants were constructed all through the house. A fire did break out in 1899, and it was largely thanks to the 'splendid equipment of fire-extinguishing apparatus', wrote the *Sussex Daily News*, that it had been brought under control by the time Chichester Fire Brigade arrived on the scene, some three hours after the alarm had been raised.

A marble niche in the entrance hall emphasises the note of sophistication of the house, and the excitement caused by the advances in science. The niche is in many ways a symbol of everything West Dean stood for, since it is also evidence of an intimate connection with royalty. It commemorates the spot from which an 'electric spark' was transmitted to Canada by Edward VII. The occasion was the opening in Montreal of a sister institution to the King Edward VII Sanatorium at Midhurst, which Edward VII visited on each of his many trips to West Dean, and of which Willie James, typically, was executive chairman. The King could not cross the Atlantic in person, so it was decided to perform the ceremony by remote control. 'The current, despatched on its way by his Majesty, travelled at an inconceivable pace,' gasped the *Daily Telegraph*. In Montreal, the 'invisible power' opened the doors, turned on the electric lights and ran the Union Jack up the flagpole. By contrast, the ceremony at West Dean was rather an anticlimax: the King simply walked out of the dining room and put his finger on something that looked like a bell-push.

Almost symbolically, the pace of life in this most Edwardian of houses began to slow up after the King's death in 1910. About that time, Mrs James began to suffer badly from heart trouble; then, in 1912, Willie James died. As a result, from 1914 to 1932 the house was let, although Mrs James lived until 1927. There was a brief recrudescence during the period that Willie James's son, Edward, was married to the dancer Tilly Losch. The house was full of artists and poets, and a whole corps de ballet stayed there for the summer of 1933, Monkton became a Surrealist caprice, filled with self-conscious weirdness. But the marriage broke down and Edward James spent increasing amounts of time in Mexico. Before his death, he turned West Dean into a foundation in memory of his parents. The main George and Peto rooms survive. The Surrealist collection and Monkton itself were sold, to become a private home of less singularity than under its Surrealist iteration.

CONSUELO VANDERBILT

AT

BLENHEIM PALACE
& CROWHURST PLACE

In 1895, Consuelo Vanderbilt found herself beside her new husband, 'Sunny', the 9th Duke of Marlborough, in a carriage that had been unhitched from the horses and was being dragged by the staff of the estate to Blenheim Palace in Oxfordshire. It was a cold day and she wore a coat of sables, beneath a big hat. As she later recalled, the speeches and ceremonies associated with the arrival of a new bride at the house seemed interminable, the coat came to feel heavier and heavier, and her hat blew about in the wind. Even the prospect of the hot bath that had been prepared for her, with a silk tea gown to slip into afterwards, could not reconcile her to the tedium. She longed to be alone. But that was not to be permitted for the chatelaine of a great country house.

PREVIOUS PAGES
Blenheim Palace, Oxfordshire, built by a grateful nation for the Duke of Marlborough after his victories against Louis XIV. After his marriage to Consuelo Vanderbilt in 1895, the 9th Duke of Marlborough had the principal rooms redecorated, ironically, in the style of Louis XIV.

John Singer Sargent's swagger portrait of The 9th Duke and Duchess of Marlborough and their two sons, painted in 1905. The use of steps was intended to disguise the Duke's relative lack of stature.

RIGHT The Duke of Marlborough (4th from left) and Consuela, Duchess of Marlborough (2nd from left) relaxing on board the P&O liner *Arabia* on its trip from Marseilles to Bombay en route to the Delhi Durbar. With the Marquess of Curzon, as Viceroy, taking the place of the King, it was the most spectacular of the Durbars.

Consuelo was not the first American to marry a Marlborough. In 1888, Sunny's father, the 8th Duke, had arrived in New York, supposedly in pursuit of a scheme to turn base metals into gold, although in reality looking for the more reliable method of transmutation – marrying a rich heiress. The Duke may have been regarded by some of his contemporaries as a brilliant individual undone by fate (and his own character failings), but he did not look like a good marital bet. Ten years earlier, his impetuous hedonism had been revealed in the glare of gleeful public scrutiny in the Aylesford divorce case, and his first wife, Albertha, a daughter of the Duke of Abercorn, had divorced him, claiming that he had struck her while she was pregnant. A likely marriage prospect, however, was spotted by Leonard Jerome, whose daughter, Jennie, had married Lord Randolph Churchill, the Duke's brother. 'I rather think he will marry the Hammersley,' he reported to his wife, after Marlborough had left for the Adirondacks; '... there is no doubt that she has lots of tin'.

Lily Hammersley had changed her name from Lilian, supposedly because she disliked the rhyme with million. Known as Lily of Troy, from her home town in New York state, she had been left immensely rich by the death of her first husband, Louis Hammersley of New York. In person, she was rather large, with a straight nose and the shadow of a moustache, which the spiteful exaggerated into a beard. Since the Duke was

divorced, there was some difficulty about finding a clergyman to perform the ceremony in New York, but a Baptist minister obliged. At Blenheim, an intimation of things to come was provided in the marital bedroom, hung with a nude portrait of the Duke's notorious mistress, Lady Colin Campbell. Lily had it destroyed, supposedly posting the pieces to Lady Colin in Venice. But putting her foot down on this occasion did not prevent the Duke from treating Lily shamefully as a matter of course. Blenheim benefited from her money, which provided new lead for the roof, as well as (influenced, perhaps, by the Duke's passion for science) central heating and electric lighting. Consuelo later found that the two electricians who ran the lighting system, one of the earliest in the country, were regarded as 'men of science', and as such on a par with the butler. But a note of pathos is struck by the inscription on the organ, commissioned from Father Willis in 1891: 'In memory of happy days and as a tribute to this glorious home, we leave thy voice to speak within these walls in years to come when ours are still.' (It was found as a note scribbled by the Duke on a scrap of paper torn from *The Times*.) Lily's days during this marriage – she married for the third time after the Duke's death in 1892 – were anything but happy.

In *The Glitter and the Gold*, published in 1952, Consuelo describes the brutal regime under which she was brought up, the culmination of which was her marriage to Sunny. She first met him at Blenheim, an impression of whose importance had been implanted even before she had so much as reached the steps of the palace, due to the appearance

'I rather think he will marry the Hammersley,' he reported to his wife, after Marlborough had left for the Adirondacks; '... there is no doubt that she has lots of tin'.

ABOVE On arriving at Blenheim, Consuelo Vanderbilt would have noticed that even some of the oak trees were many centuries old. She felt oppressed by the stuffiness of the tradition-bound Marlboroughs. The disaster of her marriage helped inspire Edith Wharton's *The Buccaneers*.

Beneath wall-
paintings by James Thornhill, the
Great Hall was, in the Edwardian
period, arranged - according to
the country-house fashion – for
separate conversational groups,
so that the different elements of
a house party could interact as
they wished. In the centre is the
inevitable potted palm.

Young, radiant, better educated than the
English girls into whose company she was thrown,
but with a long neck that nature seemed to have
designed for showing off a fashionable dog collar
of pearls, Consuelo found Blenheim to be vast,
frigid and inconvenient.

of a porter in livery carrying a wand of office, topped by a silver knob, at the lodge. From
there, she and her domineering mother Alva swept along an avenue of elms, past the lake,
beneath one arch, then another, briefly noting the hothouses that had once served as a
picture gallery (some of the classical themes of the Old Masters were thought too risqué
for female eyes). In the distance stood the column surmounted by a statue of the 1st Duke
of Marlborough, whose victories in the Seven Years War had caused a grateful nation to
bestow on him such domestic splendours. The next day, Sunday, Sunny took his guests on
a tour of the estate, past cottage gardens whose occupants respectfully touched their caps
or curtsied, according to sex. This was a world of 'ancient traditions', and Consuelo left it
determined that she would not marry the Duke. She had already become secretly engaged
to an American called Winthrop Rutherfurd.

Soon, though, Sunny crossed the Atlantic to propose. Alva brought her formidable
personality to work on her daughter, supposedly keeping her locked up so securely that
any correspondence, let alone meeting, with Rutherfurd was impossible, and using every
kind of moral blackmail to favour Sunny. After one scene, Alva apparently suffered a
heart attack and Consuelo was told that further resistance on her part would kill her. And
so, with a thick veil to hide the tears, she was driven to the altar, to find Marlborough not
meeting her eyes, but staring vacantly into space. Be warned that this was promulgated
several decades after the events concerned. By then, the marriage had not only ended
unhappily, but the need to secure an annulment in order to satisfy her second husband
Jacques Balsan's Roman Catholic family, as well as
Sunny's own adoption by the Roman Catholic Church,
had established the need to show that Consuelo had
been coerced into it. At the time, it did not seem that
Consuelo had been shut away; she attended social
events, from which she could have escaped if she
chose. What is certain is that she soon came to find
Sunny stuffy and hidebound. Blenheim seems almost
to have been a third presence in the marriage, placing
a chill on her heart.

Young, radiant, better educated than the English
girls into whose company she was thrown, but with a
long neck that nature seemed to have designed for showing off a fashionable dog collar of
pearls, Consuelo found Blenheim to be vast, frigid and inconvenient. Having entered
'an immense hall with a domed ceiling', she had to crane that long neck to see the
apotheosis of the 1st Duke above her. It was, she mused tartly,

> Strange that in so great a house there should not be one really livable room. Planned
> to impress rather than to please … Blenheim was perhaps not designed as a home …
> We slept in small rooms with high ceilings; we dined in dark rooms with high ceilings;
> we dressed in closets without ventilation; we sat in long galleries or painted saloons.

Although her bedroom was 'comparatively small', it was graced by an enormous
marble chimneypiece 'that looked to me like a tomb'. She was embarrassed to show visitors
the bedrooms containing the tapestries commemorating the victories of the 1st Duke,
because in front of the heroic figures stood metal bathtubs, with jugs for hot and cold
water. Sunny was resistant to change; perhaps, like other country-house owners, he felt it
was more luxurious for water to be carried to his room by servants, rather than discharged
from a pipe. Coming from a plutocratic American background, Consuelo was aghast.

Her democratic sensibilities also rebelled against the stiffness of the domestic
regime, typified by the butler who, when asked to light the fire that stood prepared in
the grate, felt it beneath his dignity and said he would summon the footman ('Oh, don't
trouble,' Consuelo replied, 'I will do it myself.') Only nineteen, she had to contend with
the demands of running a large staff, not to mention the elaborate rituals of the Edwardian
weekend party, in which a woman might be expected to change her clothes five times a
day. Titles and order of precedence taken by her guests had to be mastered. Her fingers
ached from the correspondence which guests expected to be written in her own hand.

Sunny saw no reason for modernisation to raise its head. He did, however, apply
himself – and some of Consuelo's father William Kissam Vanderbilt's money – to the

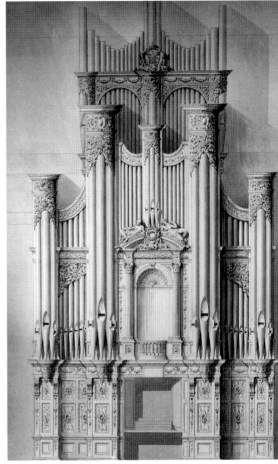

decoration of Blenheim. By the 1890s, crowded with furniture from the Marlborough's London house, the lease of which had reverted to the crown, Blenheim had lost its original clarity. The state rooms were cluttered with a grand mishmash of pieces, navigation between which was made more difficult by potted palms. This did not suit his elevated sense of the family's importance, in which his own role was merely that of a 'link in the chain', between the generations before and after. He was convinced of the palace's status as a work of art. As he wrote in 1914, 'Blenheim is the most splendid relic of the age of Anne, and there is no building in Europe, except Versailles, which so perfectly preserves its original atmosphere'.[1] He may have been conscious of being out-Versaillesed by the Rothschilds' Waddesdon Manor in Buckinghamshire, built on land that had been sold, as one of many disposals of property and treasures, by his grandfather. On inheriting – and before even having married Consuelo – he employed a French firm of interior decorators to update the state rooms in the style of the first Duke's great enemy, Louis XIV. Allegorical overdoors and gilding were the note. Reproduction French pier glasses were hung between the windows. New parquet floors were laid and then hidden beneath Aubusson or Savonnerie carpets. Avray Tipping, *Country Life*'s architectural editor, cannot have realised that the work had only been completed for a decade when he called it 'a little heavy and gorgeous' – an aspersion against ducal taste which he would hardly have risked otherwise.

Sunny later thought he had made a mistake. So did Consuelo. Sunny's nickname derived from the courtesy title Lord Sunderland that he had held as a child, not from any suggestion of brightness or warmth of disposition. Consuelo came to dread the meals alone with him, to which he often arrived late, and which were passed in moody silence as he fiddled with his signet ring and she occupied herself with knitting. In 1905, having produced two male children,

Sunny's nickname derived from the courtesy title Lord Sunderland that he had held as a child, not from any suggestion of brightness or warmth of disposition

RIGHT The 9th Duke laid out the magnificent parterres at Blenheim to the designs of the French landscape architect Achille Duchêne.

ABOVE Brass helmets and boaters: an Edwardian fire brigade rally in the grounds of Blenheim Palace.

she effectively ended the marriage (in an episode that is overlooked in *The Glitter and the Gold*) by fleeing to Paris with her married lover Charley Castlereagh, a practised seducer of women who became Marquess of Londonderry. Sunny had already taken up with another American, one famous for beauty rather than 'lots of tin': Gladys Deacon (for whom Consuelo also seems to have felt a rather heady devotion, to judge from her letters[2]). Sunny and Gladys had met during Consuelo's convalescence after the difficult birth of her first son. A pair of sphinxes were carved with Gladys's features. These were placed on the lower terrace, part of the formal landscape by Achille Duchêne, which Sunny financed from the Vanderbilt marriage settlement that he continued to receive after the separation and eventual divorce from Consuelo. In 1921 Sunny married Gladys. But in a quest to perfect her almost ideal Grecian beauty she had resorted to an early form of cosmetic surgery, by which wax was injected to straighten the line of her nose. The wax slipped. Gladys became a gargoyle and an eccentric recluse, dining with a pistol beside her plate and eventually given the run of Blenheim, alone except for dozens of Blenheim spaniels who were given free rein, to the detriment of the soft furnishings.

From Blenheim, Consuelo, when not at Sunderland House – the London residence which she and Sunny had built, and which she kept as part of the divorce settlement - escaped to more congenial architectural surroundings. At Marble House at Newport, Rhode Island, her bedroom had been the only Tudor-style room in the house. Perhaps that indicates a natural taste. Certainly it was Tudor that she enthusiastically embraced at Crowhurst Place in Surrey, bought in 1912. For the previous five years, it had been home to the decorator-cum-architect George Crawley, who had also worked on Long Island, designing Westbury House for John Phipps, heir to a steel fortune. Like many old manor houses, Crowhurst had fallen down the social scale in the eighteenth and nineteenth centuries, becoming no more than a decrepit farmhouse. The process of restoration tolled on Crawley's wife – hence the sale, in 1912, to Consuelo. She continued the work,

which included enlargement in a romantic style, so sensitive to texture that they look more like the product of a watercolourist than a conventional builder. In the end, about half the house was rebuilt or raised from new above old foundations, the rest restored. The intensely poetic result could hardly have been more different from Blenheim.

'With its high roof of Horsham stone, its walls half-timbered with silvered oak, its stone chimneys and leaded casements, it had the charm of an old engraving. It was, I thought, a dream come true.'[3] In *Country Life*, Crowhurst received an accolade from the mountaineer, art historian and peer Martin Conway (1st Baron Conway of Allington), who had meticulously restored Allington Castle in Kent. The repairs had not muddled the history of the building but made it more evident. On a more practical note, nobody could have hesitated 'to pronounce the house as it now stands an abode comfortable to dwell in'. The tone was set by Consuelo's 'indubitably picturesque' sitting room, 'with its lining of faintly coloured and patchily gilt linenfold panelling of the French type' and walls 'frankly "faked" to look old'. To Conway, it had 'the aspect of a pleasant retiring place, where one might read or dream in peace through the quiet hours of a summer's day'.

'It had the aspect of a pleasant retiring place, where one might read or dream in peace through the quiet hours of a summer's day'.

In the summer of 1919, Crowhurst received an enthusiastic endorsement from the smouldering, panther-like Grand Duke Dmitry Pavlovich Romanov who found it 'one of the most beautiful places I've ever seen' – but then he was either having or hoped to have an affair with his hostess. Whatever Dmitry's role in Consuelo's life, it was soon eclipsed by the equally dashing Balsan. In 1921, he and Consuelo married: another dream came true – for Balsan at least, since he had told his mother than he wanted to wed Consuelo on first seeing her in the 1890s. Later, they took the furniture from Crowhurst to the house that Duchêne built for them in the South of France.

ABOVE The Tudor charm of
Crowhurst Place, Surrey,
heightened by the antiquarian
George Crawley in the Edwardian
period, could not have been a
greater contrast to the frigid
grandeur of Blenheim. Consuelo
Vanderbilt retreated here after her
divorce from the Duke.

RIGHT Consuelo married as her
second husband the Frenchman
Jacques Balsan. She is shown here
sitting with him, perhaps in the
house which Achille Duchêne built
for them in the South of France.

RIGHT Consuelo Vanderbilt's parlour at Crowhurst, in a new extension to the house. 'The little sitting-room with its lining of faintly coloured and patchily gilt linenfold panelling of a French type is indubitably picturesque,' opined the connoisseur Martin Conway in *Country Life*, July 12, 1919. He was, however, doubtful about the ceiling, with its less subtle colours.

BELOW The Dutch garden at Crowhurst Place. Martin Conway concluded that Consuelo and her architect George Crawley had not merely rescued the 'battered remains' of a medieval house from neglect, but brought Crowhurst to a state of 'beauty probably far greater than' it ever had 'in the day of its newness'.

ANDREW CARNEGIE

AT

SKIBO CASTLE

In 1897, Louise Carnegie bought a present for her husband, the former steel boss-turned-philanthropist, Andrew. It was the cottage where he had been born in the Fife town of Dunfermline sixty-two years earlier. The year 1897 was also the one in which Carnegie, searching for a country house in the north of Scotland, was taken by wagonette to the 32,000-acre Skibo estate. After the carriage had jogged along beside a shining stretch of water which sometimes came quite close to it, past a precipitous bank, through meadows grazed by sheep and cattle that were dotted with farmhouses, by a wooded hill, beyond which stretched heather-clad moors as far as the eye could see, they came to an unremarkable nineteenth-century house and saw the Dornoch Firth. 'There's just the place for my yacht,' exclaimed the plutocrat. The existing structure disappeared beneath the envelope of a huge baronial structure, bulging with towers and turrets and fretted with crow-stepped gables. The new Skibo Castle was a statement of Carnegie's success.

The cottage, the castle: no man in Britain has left a more vivid architectural picture of his life's journey. The cottage had been poor; Andrew's parents wove linen damask at a time when automated looms and the factory system were pricing their hand skills out of the market. In 1848, the family emigrated to the United States. There Andrew became a bobbin winder, then telegraph operator. It set him on the path to becoming a railway magnate and finally the Steel King of America. He sold his Carnegie Steel Company in 1901 for the astonishing figure of $400 million – upon which he threw himself into a second career of philanthropy in which most of his fortune was given away. By the time of his death in 1919, 2,509 towns throughout the English-speaking world (380 in Britain) had received a library endowed by Carnegie – Dunfermline naturally being the first.

The world in which Carnegie made his fortune had been ruthlessly competitive, and at first glance Skibo may be thought to reflect the harsh side of his personality. The architects, Ross and Macbeth, came from the city nearest to Skibo, Inverness. The senior partner, Dr Alexander Ross, was an old-fashioned Victorian who had done very well out of the Highland boom of the 1850s and 1860s, building houses and shooting lodges as well as schools and – his magnum opus – Inverness Cathedral. With the efficiency of a businessman, Carnegie delegated the planning of the castle to Louise, who was inclined to be overawed by her husband's expectations, while the improvement of the estate was left to his factor. Skibo is not a thing of great subtlety, although the pinkish granite is well cut and the decoration – beasts over the window and thistles on the skyline – is restrained.

But if the result is at times elephantine, the conception was personal and touching. Previously, the Carnegies had rented Cluny Castle in Aberdeenshire, which they considered pretty well perfect, in a setting that was, wrote Louise, 'just like the scenery in *Die Walküre*'.[1] It was the birth of their daughter Margaret that inspired them to build. As Carnegie remembered, Louise, who had turned forty a few weeks earlier, raised the subject as soon as he went into the bedroom to greet his daughter for the first time. 'Here, Andrew, is your daughter,' she began.

'Her name is Margaret after your mother. Now, one request I have to make.'

'What is it, Lou?'

'We must get a summer home since this little one has been given to us. We cannot any longer rent one and be obliged to go in and go out at a certain date. It should be our home.'

'Yes,' he agreed.

He made only one condition.

'What is that?' she asked.

'It must be in the Highlands of Scotland.'[2]

When Andrew went off to explore the Duke of Sutherland's vast domain to fulfil his wife's dream, Louise understandably developed cold feet as to the choice that her strong-willed husband might make. 'Am very anxious too for your report by word of mouth,' she wrote in a letter.

We now want to take root. We haven't time to make mistakes; as many playthings and playplaces as you like and yachts galore, but a home first please, where we can have the greatest measure of health ... I'll try to be happy wherever you settle. We shall gang far ere we find anything muckle better than Cluny for baby. Her cheeks are as brown and as fat as possible. She almost talked to me as I was undressing her this evening.[3]

Lou was perhaps right to be apprehensive. Summer home it may have been, but the scale required of a building that also befitted Carnegie's status as a self-made radical, with more than one lesson that he felt he should teach the world, who entertained statesmen and royalty, meant that it became a very big one.

While some of the time spent at Skibo was passed by its occupants in a family setting, the architectural leviathan that Carnegie had created could still be oppressive, and he and his family would escape, first to a comparatively primitive stone cottage, Achinduich, and then a large house built for the same simple existence, Altnager Lodge. Neither Carnegie nor his Louise was especially interested in architecture or the trappings of a great house.

The inner Carnegie was rarely glimpsed by his political guests, to whom his manner was heavily jocose, hectoring, obstreperous. He dressed as a pantomime laird, in

Norfolk suits of patterns loud enough to be heard a good league into the Atlantic, shooting-coats of plaid tweed, chequered on so large a scale as to do duty for chess-boards, coaching attire that might have taken away the elder Weller's breath, with mother-of-pearl buttons the size of saucers, like those once affected by our own Mr. Cherry Angell.[4]

Powerful Liberal politicians like Lloyd George, and John Morley, cabinet minister, biographer of Gladstone and Carnegie's particular friend, rubbed shoulders with university professors, American businessmen, local worthies, neighbours from Dunfermline, and Rudyard Kipling. To celebrate the completion of the house, the King himself came to luncheon. Carnegie received him in the library and read a poem composed for his birthday by Joaquin Miller, 'the poet of the Sierras'. The opening lines included the invocation 'Hail, fat Edward!' which, with heavy humour, Carnegie underlined by saying, 'That's you, Sir.' It went down like a stone.

On the balustrade of the terrace constructed on the south side of the house, they carved the words 'I will lift up mine eyes unto the hills': a testimony to the view across the Dornoch Firth to the hills of Ross that had drawn them to this spot in the first place, and remained its greatest charm. Like other plutocrats, particularly in the United States, Carnegie enjoyed controlling the power of a team of horses, driving a carriage four-in-hand. To be relished at its best, the sport required a country estate, with better road

The world in which Carnegie made his fortune had been ruthlessly competitive, and at first glance Skibo may be thought to reflect the harsh side of his personality.

ABOVE The hall was built on a titanic scale, with player organ, Sicilian marble staircase and a stained glass window telling the story of Skibo and Carnegie's life.

Summer home it may have been, but the scale required of a building that also befitted Carnegie's status as a self-made radical...

surfaces than those of a rutted and potholed Highland lane. There was no more beautifully wooded estate than Skibo – almost every tree of which was sacrificed to the government when Britain was revealed as woefully short of timber during the First World War.

A contemporary estimate had it that Carnegie spent £100,000 on creating the present Skibo. Two hundred tons of steel from Carnegie's Pittsburg steelworks were used in the alterations. Visitors would arrive, as Louise Carnegie described, through 'a beautiful undulating park with cattle grazing, a stately avenue of fine old beeches, glimpses of the Dornoch Firth, about a mile away, all seen through the picturesque cluster of lime and beech trees'.[5] Probably on the advice of the landscape architect Thomas Mawson, Carnegie dammed three rivers to make lochs.

The house is planned around the hall, panelled in dark fumed oak and hung with trophies of stags and moose. A broad staircase of Sicilian marble sweeps down next to the organ, and over the landing is a big stained-glass window by Gerald Moira telling the story of the house and Carnegie's own fairy tale of capitalist endeavour. It was typical of Carnegie's didactic interest in history. The inner lights show owners of the previous house on the site – the thirteenth-century Bishop Gilbert of Dornoch, the Viking chief Sigurd – and the Marquess of Montrose, imprisoned at Skibo in 1650. The outer lights depict, on the left-hand side, the humble cottage in which Carnegie was born and the sailing ship which first took his impoverished family to America when he was a child. On the right-hand side is the liner on which, years later, he made his return – shown steaming out of

It used to be said that the hen house at Skibo was better than any dwelling house at Dornoch, because the hen house had electric lighting.

New York harbour with the Statue of Liberty in the background – and, below, Skibo Castle itself, pink, glittering and the symbol of self-made triumph. The library was handsomely appointed with a book collection recommended by Lord Acton, whose own library was perhaps the greatest in Europe – too handsomely for Carnegie's taste, since the factor had the volumes rebound to reflect their setting, an expense Carnegie thought completely unwarranted and apt to detract from the wisdom found within their pages. Alas, the books seem to have been little read. Guests may be forgiven for being distracted, given the variety of outdoor activities on offer: fishing, yachting, golf, even shooting, although Carnegie himself never participated, on principle.

It used to be said that the hen house at Skibo was better than any dwelling house at Dornoch, because the hen house had electric lighting. The big power house constructed towards the loch had a long underground chimney to prevent smoke blowing back on to the house higher up. But the real luxury at Skibo was the swimming pool – a big stone building, with capitals of lizards and leaves. It was roofed in glass and iron like a conservatory, but the pool itself was made out of marble. The seawater for swimming was heated. The main space was big enough to double up as a ballroom when the pool was covered over with a dance floor. 'Huge electric arc lamps and chandeliers glittered overhead,' remembered one visitor. 'Tubs of evergreens were spaced along the walls, and festoons of coloured paper chains and bunting hung overhead … Mrs Logan's dance band from Inverness played in the balcony, varied by bagpipe music for Scotch Reels, Eightsome Reels, Highland Scottische and so forth, played so harmoniously by the Castle piper.' Mawson thought the costly structure introduced 'a persistent jarring note'.

After Carnegie's death in 1919, Skibo continued in his family, beautifully kept up but used, eventually, for only a few weeks a year. Architecturally, it had a renaissance when it was turned into a private club-cum-hotel, performing a not dissimilar function from the one for which it was planned.

ABOVE The eminent scholar Lord Acton chose the books for the library. The factor got into trouble for having them expensively rebound: Carnegie wanted to give the impression of a working library although in practice the books were rarely opened.

RIGHT The Swimming pool, which, to the landscape architect Thomas Mawson, introduced 'a persistent jarring note'. It could be floored over to serve as a ballroom.

MAY GOELET

AT

FLOORS CASTLE

In the winter of 1902, May Goelet was having a good time. 'I can't begin to tell you what fun I had in London,' wrote the twenty-two-year-old. 'It simply was glorious. You know how fond I am of dancing, and all my old partners were so kind to me, and I made several new ones.' She was in the marriage market – or was thought to be – and enjoying every minute of the fascination in which she was held by the male sex. The letter to her Aunt Grace Vanderbilt, written from Bad Homburg, the spa frequented by Edward VII, makes it sound like rather a game:

PREVIOUS PAGES Rich, vivacious, slim-waisted: May Goelet had no shortage of admirers to disappoint when she married the 8th Duke of Roxburghe.

Floors Castle: the vision of Scottish Baronial pageantry that greets travellers crossing the Tweed into Scotland at Kelso. To many people's surprise, May Goelet, who married the 8th Duke of Roxburghe in 1903, settled contentedly in the Borders and made an exemplary Duchess.

I must give an account of my proposals. Well, first Lord Shaftsbury [sic] popped almost as soon as he returned to London. He came one afternoon. Mamma happened to leave the room for a few minutes and off he went – like a pistol. I told him it was quite ridiculous as he had only known me three weeks and he couldn't possibly know his own mind – and besides I knew nothing of him nor his past beyond the fact that when he was 21 he had been devoted to Lady N—, which he said was true that was all over long ago – and he was certain he knew his own mind. I like him very much only I have no intention of marrying him or anyone else at present.

Even so, May's mother, also called May, was 'terribly afraid' that her daughter would accept Lord Shaftesbury. Popular opinion had it that she was already engaged to the Duke of Roxburghe, whose seat of Floors Castle, just over the Scottish border, stood on an estate of over 60,000 acres, although she 'didn't see him at all at first as he never goes to balls'. May did, however, meet him 'at Mrs James'', presumably Mrs Willie James of West Dean, when 'he came and talked to me and the following night we met at Lady Curzon's where we were dining'. She described it as: 'Such a nice dinner. Lord Castlereagh took me in (the Londonderry boy) and we talked together afterwards so I didn't have a chance of saying a word to the Duke.'

OPPOSITE The trunks, portmanteaux, dress baskets and suitcases that contained May Goelet's substantial trousseau on her marriage to the 8th Duke of Roxburghe in 1903. She also brought a dowry of some $20 million.

RIGHT A page from *The Sketch* September 23, 1903, shortly before May Goelet married 'Bumble', the 8th Duke of Roxburghe. May wears an exotic and opulent ballgown, while Bumble is dressed in the uniform of the Household Cavalry. He loved shooting, polo, horses, golf and May.

AMERICA AND THE PEERAGE.

(SEE "SMALL TALK OF THE WEEK.")

[*Photograph by Thomson, Grosvenor Street, W.*]

MISS MAY GOELET.

[*Photograph by Mayall, Piccadilly.*]

THE DUKE OF ROXBURGHE.

WHOSE WEDDING WILL SHORTLY TAKE PLACE.

Mrs Goelet should have been grateful that May escaped Charley Castlereagh's clutches: he was a hopeless womaniser, whose affair with Consuelo Marlborough would end her marriage to the 9th Duke.

Meanwhile, friends of Captain George Holford, owner of Dorchester House on Park Lane (later replaced by the Dorchester Hotel), thought he would be a suitable partner. Holford's brother-in-law, Lord Grey, was 'very anxious to arrange it', and even the Prince of Wales – whose qualifications as a marriage broker might be doubted – took a view:

The prince said to Lord Grey, 'It's quite time George (Captain H.) was getting married. I know just the right person for him – a charming girl, Miss Goelet. It really must be arranged.

Holford himself hesitated, wanting to find out the lie of the land before making

OPPOSITE The forest of pinnacles, chimneystacks and turrets that enlivens the skyline of Floors Castle. May's dowry enabled the Duke to modernise the castle with the installation of electric light, central heating and proper drains.

RIGHT The smart decorators Lenygon and Morant were commissioned to bring Floors Castle up to date. Their spell was not only cast over the castle's main rooms, but its plumbing: this bathroom is in the fashionable Louis XVI style that was identified with the contemporary Ritz Hotel in London. There were, of course, no bathrooms in eighteenth-century France.

She was beautiful, vivacious (she possessed the 'three natural attributes of the American girl', being 'bright, amusing and quick') – and her father was very rich.

an embarrassment of himself, but May had already decided that he would not do. 'Dorchester House, of course, would be delightful and I believe he has two charming places in the country. Unfortunately, the dear man has no title, though a very good position – and I am sure he would make a very good husband.'

The final offer on the list came from the charming, impecunious George Cornwallis-West. 'Such a dear, attractive, good-looking boy, and quite the best dancer in London.' He was smitten. George's sister, Princess Henry of Pless, otherwise known as Daisy, did not see what all the fuss was about. 'How I should hate to be May Goelet,' she wrote in her diary, 'all those odious little Frenchmen, and dozens of others, crowding round her millions.'[1] But her viewpoint was that of a young woman who had already been married off at eighteen to a rich European prince. One detects the taste of sour grapes. May saw Cornwallis-West as another admirer she would disappoint, although:

> He fancies himself very much in love with me. So foolish of him. I am so sorry about it – but what can one do? I like him ever so much as a friend – but why they have always to wish for something more, I can't imagine.[2]

If she could not imagine, others had no difficulty in doing so. She was beautiful, vivacious (she possessed the 'three natural attributes of the American girl', being 'bright, amusing and quick'[3]) – and her father was very rich.

The Goelet fortune, mostly in New York real estate, was second only to the Astors'. Ogden Goelet – Ogden was May's father – died on his yacht *The Mayflower* at Cowes in

A flavour of the evening was that the 'cotillion favours' – or, as they might be known today, going-home presents – were specially made by Tiffany in silver.

1899; he left a fortune of $60 million, as did his brother Robert.[4] They had upset the old social order by the freedom with which they spent. In 1884, Mrs Ogden Goelet had thrown open the doors of the family's Fifth Avenue mansion for a spectacular ball in rooms opulently panelled and lined with rich tapestries. A flavour of the evening was that the 'cotillion favours' – or, as they might be known today, going-home presents – were specially made by Tiffany in silver. This initiated the period characterised by the American economist Thorstein Veblen as that of 'conspicuous consumption' – or showing off for the sake of it. Although May Goelet had been 'carefully brought up, and had the best teachers for languages, music, riding and fencing',[5] her background was not a sequestered one. Her father spent most of his last years abroad, more than once entertaining the Prince of Wales. About the time of his death from a weak heart in 1897, May, in her teens, had a close shave with the appalling Duke of Manchester, who overplayed his hand by announcing their engagement and was finally seen off.[6] Consuelo Vanderbilt took her under her wing, asking her to be the bridesmaid at her wedding to 'Sunny' Marlborough in 1895. Radiant but well versed in the ways of the world, this captivating girl knew exactly what she was about.

The prize eventually fell to the reticent, serious-minded 8th Duke of Roxburghe. He and May married in 1903. Thereupon, however difficult it might have been to predict from her time in London as a suitable marriage prospect, May settled down to the life of a Duchess in a draughty castle on the River Tweed. Her money may have allowed the usual electricity and bathrooms to be installed, but it must still have seemed – both geographically and in terms of comfort – a long way from the luxurious homes she had known in New York and Newport, Rhode Island. Nevertheless, they made – unusually in such circles – a devoted couple.

The Duke had been sixteen when he came into his title. He was remembered, in his *Times* obituary,[7] as 'an admirable landlord', who 'fulfilled all the duties of his position', as well as being good soldier who 'behaved with conspicuous gallantry' in the Boer War. He was severely wounded during the First World War in 1914. Fifteen years before his death, he became ordained, serving as an elder of Kelso old parish church. He and the Duchess were friends of George V and Queen Mary. Generally, he was everything that could be hoped from a Duke: brave, worthy, conscientious, albeit rather dull, as might be judged from his affectionate nickname 'Bumble'. May, after what must have been a rather anxious wait for an heir – their only child, George, the Marquess of Bowmont, was born in 1913 – was everything that could be hoped of a Duchess. Her liveliness continued to raise eyebrows: after Bumble's death in 1932, she took up flying.

Floors Castle was an enormous, spreading country house, the sight of which, with a legion of lead-capped pinnacles glinting on the skyline, never fails to inspire the architectural historian Marcus Binney with 'awe'.[8] To Sir Walter Scott, Floors may have been modern, but it did not lack romance: 'With its terrace, its woods, and its extensive lawn, [it] forms altogether a kingdom for Oberon or Titania to dwell in.' Contemporaries might well have thought that May and Floors were made for each other.

It had been begun by the brilliant 5th Earl of Roxburghe, described even by a political enemy as 'the best accomplish'd young man of quality in Europe', in the early eighteenth century, after Lord Roxburghe had supported the Union of Scotland with England in 1707. The architect was William Adam, father of Robert. Adam produced a rather plain building; the fantasy of the castle to which the 8th Duke brought his American bride had been provided by William Playfair, in a kind of rhapsody on a baronial theme. All those pinnacles are grouped with towers, turrets, crow-stepped gables, ogee roofs and a profusion of ornament.

May's father having died four years before the marriage, she not only brought with her a very splendid dowry but a sumptuous collection of French furniture which had found its way into Goelet homes on the other side of the Atlantic. This included some top-quality French furniture and a set of magnificent tapestries. The main rooms at Floors were remodelled, probably by the fashionable decorating firm of Lenygon and Morant, to receive these treasures. The rise of the interior decorator was a late Victorian phenomenon. Lenygon and Morant could supply not only some of the most sybaritic of soft furnishing – deeply sprung, elaborately fringed, upholstered in the most gorgeous fabrics, sometimes with antique panels set into the backs of chairs and sofas – but also craftsmanship of the highest standard. In smart country houses taste was generally eclectic, with different period styles being used for different rooms – French for drawing rooms, English for dining rooms, Early for halls and so on. The repertoire at Floors was restricted to the eighteenth century, but with variations on that general theme: the drawing room became Louis Quinze; the Needle Room Louis Seize; the ballroom, hung with a superb series of Gobelins tapestries, George I; with swags in the manner of Grinling Gibbons carved by a local man, the Duchess's drawing room George I. One of the bathrooms was panelled in the Louis XVI style associated with the Ritz Hotel. A late thought was to build a pair of elegant entrance lodges, with bell-shaped roofs, in 1929; they were designed by Reginald Fairlie.

There is still a Duke and Duchess of Roxburghe in residence at Floors, which remains, in part, a testament to the 8th Duke's happy marriage.

'With its terrace, its woods, and its extensive lawn, [it] forms altogether a kingdom for Oberon or Titania to dwell in.'

PREVIOUS PAGES The entrance front of Floors Castle, which is flanked to either side by large courts for stables and services. To travellers crossing the Tweed at Kelso, it is their first sight of Scotland.

OPPOSITE One of the delicious rooms – in this case, painted apple green – which the decorators Lenygon and Morant created for the Roxburghes. Not only did May enjoy collecting works of art, but she came to inherit important collections from America. The tapestries in the Drawing Room were incorporated into a set of new panelling with a sumptuous marble fireplace in 1930.

WILFRED & BERTHA BUCKLEY

AT

MOUNDSMERE MANOR

Wilfred Buckley came from Birmingham, but his family had strong transatlantic leanings. His father, Henry Buckley, ran a shipping company, which exported manufactured goods; his mother, Caroline Kennard, came from Massachusetts, where her father worked for a jewellery firm. Wilfred's two brothers emigrated, one to Florida, the other to British Columbia, leaving Wilfred to work in the family firm. When he was sent to represent it in the United States, living on a humble salary, he managed to catch the eye of Bertha Terrell, a wealthy heiress whose family had originally come from Cleveland, Ohio, but had graduated to houses on Fifth Avenue and in Seabright, New Jersey. They married in 1898, and, five years later, Wilfred took his bride and young daughter to live in England. His father had died and he now had to run the firm by himself.

PREVIOUS PAGES
The entrance front of Moundsmere Manor, Hampshire, built for Wilfred Buckley by Sir Reginald Blomfield in 1907–8. It is modelled on Wren's wing at Hampton Court Palace.

Wilfred Buckley, businessman and pioneer of safe milk.

In 1905, Bertha fell ill with an infection of the tubercular glands. Tuberculosis was somewhat better understood then than it had been in the earlier Victorian age, although it nonetheless remained a scourge. Doctors now realised that fresh air and sunshine helped destroy the bacillus – an advance which had a profound effect on the design of the Edwardian country house, opening it up to light and air, and providing it with a host of loggias, outdoor sleeping balconies and garden rooms. It turned the Buckleys' mind towards acquiring a country property, which they did the next year; in 1907-09 they employed Sir Reginald Blomfield to build them Moundsmere Manor, near Basingstoke in Hampshire, in the style of Wren's wing at Hampton Court Palace in Surrey.

One of the features of country houses – in what was known in the United States as the Gilded Age and that the Buckleys would have noted there – was the farm group. In Britain, this was called the model farm. The great age of the model farm in Britain had

ABOVE The hall at Moundsmere, decorated in English Renaissance style. Buckley had married an heiress while in New York, representing the family firm.

LEFT Early Georgian furniture in the dining room of Moundsmere.

In 1907–09 they employed Sir Reginald Blomfield to build them Moundsmere Manor, near Basingstoke in Hampshire, in the style of Wren's wing at Hampton Court Palace.

peaked a century earlier, when landowners such as the 5th Duke of Bedford and Coke of Norfolk (the 1st Earl of Leicester) were demonstrating best practice to their neighbours during the Agricultural Revolution. In Britain, the middle years of the nineteenth century had seen the High Farming movement, when agriculturalists sank large sums of money into building expansive farmsteads that were run along factory lines. Since the agricultural depression that started in the 1870s, the idea of the model farm as an agricultural showcase had lost its lustre. This was not, however, the case on the other side of the Atlantic. There, farming was doing well. And besides, rich industrialists who built mansions outside the big cities wanted to give the appearance of farming. They did not farm for profit: they enjoyed their farms as the backdrop to their new (part-time) rural existence, as well as the cachet of having fresh eggs and vegetables sent hundreds if not thousands of miles from the farm to the city or resort houses. They also wanted clean milk.

The US was quicker to respond to the condition of milk than Britain was, in part a reflection of the depressed nature of British farming. With low wheat prices, many arable farmers converted their land to dairy farming, in order to supply the ever-expanding urban market. They were not necessarily good stockmen, and nor was there a basic understanding of the principles of hygiene on the farm. Beasts and farmyards were not always kept clean, with the result that muck often got into the milk. The worst of it was filtered out, but the meshes used in the process left some detritus still floating – and that was only what was visible. A survey of milk sold in London in 1912, conducted by *Country Life*, revealed that some of it was swimming with foreign matter. Wilfred Buckley took a leading role in the campaign to improve standards.

At Moundsmere, he took the farm in hand. Previously, the tenant had kept few records and so could neither tell how well the farm was doing nor how he could improve its running. Buckley introduced business principles, expanding from sheep into pigs, poultry and, above all, a dairy herd. New barns were

ABOVE & RIGHT Pure milk became a concern for the Buckleys after Mrs Buckley developed early tuberculosis. Wilfred campaigned on the subject, demonstrating best practice through his TB-free herd.

built along efficient lines (using concrete and metal pipes for easy cleaning). Dressed in white, the milkers had to keep their fingernails short and the cows clean. Milking buckets were sterilised after use. What had begun as an enterprise to provide clean milk for the family grew into a business that could sell the surplus in London. It might have been twice the price of other milk, but there was a market for it, including one at Buckingham Palace. Buckley became an energetic correspondent to the newspapers. In 1914 he acquired political support for a Milk and Dairies Bill to introduce the certification of milk. The sponsor was Waldorf Astor, also from an American family, who had a model dairy at Cliveden. From 1917 to 1919, Buckley served as Director of Milk Supplies at the Ministry of Food.

Bertha was actively engaged in Wilfred's farming interests, becoming her husband's 'enthusiastic colleague'; she frequently lectured in Hampshire and elsewhere on the importance of clean milk. Visiting friends were exposed to the full force of the passion. But after an hour or two of 'the milk subject', they might be shown his collection of old glass: after her husband's death, Bertha, who completed the catalogue, loaned it in perpetuity to the Victoria and Albert Museum. It was perhaps, observed her obituary in *The Times*, 'the finest private collection in the country'. Wilfred died in 1933. Bertha, described as 'at all ages lovely to look at, with her white hair, which had been so since her twenties, and her fine, clear skin and delicate colouring', had been an energetic lady of the manor, but sold Moundsmere a year before her own death in 1937. It is still, however, to this day a private home.

What had begun as an enterprise to provide clean milk for the family grew into a business that could sell the surplus in London.

LEFT Wilfred and Bertha Buckley in the grounds of Moundsmere around 1930. During the 1930s, Buckley continued to lobby the government about improving the quality of milk. However, his affairs were overshadowed by the suicide of the Swedish financier Ivar Kreuger and the collapse of his business empire, in which Buckley lost heavily.

BELOW Bertha Buckley (centre) and daughter Janet Buckley (left) in the gardens at Moundsmere in the mid-1920s, with an unnamed American guest. Like her parents, Janet was altruistic. She worked for a time in an East End soup kitchen and is supposed to have brought homeless people back to Moundsmere for a bath and a square meal when she met them in the lanes of Hampshire.

LAWRENCE JOHNSTON

AT

HIDCOTE MANOR

U ntil the early twentieth century, a farmhouse stood at Hidcote Bartrim, on the northern escarpment of the Cotswolds in Gloucestershire. In 1907, it was bought by a cultivated, rich and formidable New Yorker called Mrs Gertrude Winthrop, for her son by her first marriage, Lawrence Johnston. Johnston was thirty-six. He had not as yet shown any particular aptitude in life, but now he found his métier. He created one of England's most beautiful gardens. The farmhouse moved up the social scale to become Hidcote Manor.

Gertrude Johnston, as she then was, had been one of those Henry James-type Americans who were drawn to the art, culture and architecture of Europe, particularly belle époque France. Lawrence was born in Paris and spent his childhood there, the influence of which survived in the rolled 'r' of his accent. His parents being foreigners of means, he was educated at home with a tutor. At some point he became a Roman Catholic, but he transferred his affection to England, going up to Trinity College, Cambridge, at the late age of twenty-three; he graduated in 1897. Three years later, he became a naturalised British citizen and demonstrated his loyalty to his adopted homeland by joining the Imperial Yeomanry to fight in the Boer War. A reserved man, whose later tastes seem to have been wholly horticultural and artistic, gentle and comfort loving, he seems an unlikely soldier. Did he join up out of a desire for adventure – or perhaps to escape the influence of his mother? He was close to her, but she was a strong personality who never loosened her grip on the purse strings, fretting that her son was a 'waster'.

On his return from the Boer War, Johnston lived in Northumberland. He had a weak chest and the northern air was thought to be bracing. He also had a friend there, Savile Clayton, whom he had met in South Africa. He studied farming; Mrs Winthrop may have imagined that he would farm the 280 acres at Hidcote. He was certainly sometimes to be seen ploughing – turning his eyes, as he did so, to the glorious view over the Vale of Evesham, away to the Malvern Hills in Worcestershire.

The Cotswolds in those days were remote, rural and poor, and farming had been in the doldrums since the 1870s. These factors may have been discouraging to an agriculturalist, but had proved highly attractive to a set with whom Johnston may have found sympathy: followers and leading lights of the Arts and Crafts movement. William Morris himself made his home at Kelmscott Manor, the old grey house which 'had grown up out of the soil'; C. R. Ashbee led his Guild of Handicraft out of the East End of London to descend on Chipping Campden; and Ernest Gimson and the brothers Ernest and Sidney Barnsley formed a community of craftsmen at Sapperton, attracted by the survival of pre-industrial traditions in this old-fashioned part of the world. The village of Broadway lay at the bottom of the escarpment on which Hidcote stood: it had been attracting American artists and writers since the 1880s. The beautiful American actress Mary Anderson had settled there with her Italian husband Antonio de Navarro. Before long, Johnston had developed a passion for gardening, to which he devoted the rest of his life.

What were Johnston's influences? Frustratingly little is known about them. Perhaps the architect Charles Edward Bateman helped plant the seed. Based in Birmingham, Bateman specialised in solidly built houses for the middle classes, his work having an Arts and Crafts flavour; he knew the Cotswolds vernacular well and worked on a number of old Cotswolds buildings, including, from 1910, the Lygon Arms at Broadway. Johnston employed him to refashion the Hidcote farmhouse into a gentleman's residence, adding a wing for his mother and turning the old farmyard into a respectable courtyard. Cottages were renovated and more built and a barn was converted into a chapel. Bateman and Johnston must have discussed domestic architecture to some extent.

It would have been natural for Bateman to have raised the garden as an issue: advanced Edwardian architects saw it as being part of an aesthetic unity with the house. Reginald Blomfield had propounded the idea

Johnston was thirty-six. He had not as yet shown any particular aptitude in life, but now he found his métier. He created one of England's most beautiful gardens.

in *Formal Gardens in England* as long ago as 1892; since then it had been made manifest in the work of Gertrude Jekyll and Edwin Lutyens. Jekyll's presence was inescapable to anyone who read *Country Life* or *The Garden*, let alone her own books. Johnston would also have known Thomas Mawson's *The Art and Craft of Garden Making*, first published in 1901, which championed gardening as 'a means of serious art expression', whose object was to create 'one harmonious comprehensive whole'. Johnston's garden had a strongly architectural character, à la Mawson, with the clipped hedges Mawson admired in his book. Hedges, used to divide a garden into compartments, were a feature of Tudor gardens, and it may be significant that in 1908 Johnson borrowed Alicia Amherst's *History of Gardening in England* (1895) from the Royal Horticultural Society's Library. But Johnston had also at some point picked up the paintbrush to become a talented flower painter; he progressed from two dimensions to three, becoming an artist of the garden, as Mawson prescribed.

Johnston had also at some point picked up the paintbrush to become a talented flower painter; he progressed from two dimensions to three, becoming an artist of the garden, as Mawson prescribed.

LEFT Lawrence Johnston was not only a gardener of genius but, as this illustration shows, a talented flower painter. Like Gertrude Jekyll, he brought the eye of an artist to his garden projects. While the profusion of this painting was inspired by Dutch flower pictures from the seventeenth century, the sense of natural luxuriance, within a tightly defined border, was one that he hoped to achieve at Hidcote.

RIGHT A perennial border in the Old Garden at Hidcote Manor Garden.

ABOVE The Phlox Garden, or White Garden, planted with white summer-flowering phlox and plants with silver foliage, which contrast with the dark green of the topiary and borders. It predates the famous White Garden at Sissinghurst.

LEFT Frank Adams, head gardener, and (with dogs) Lawrence Johnston. Both men were consumed by their passion for gardening.

FOLLOWING PAGES The long walk, looking towards two Cotswold stone summer houses and a wrought-iron grille.

Beyond an ancient cedar of Lebanon and a clump of fine beech trees, there was no garden at Hidcote when Johnston began work on it. Little by little the rough pasture was organised into a series of enclosures; the gardener Alvida Lees-Milne, a friend of Johnston, counted twenty-two of them, excluding the Beech Allée, the Lime Avenue and the Holly Avenue. Architectural gardens were not, at this date, something new, but, as Mrs Lees-Milne wrote in the magazine *Hortus*,

> Lawrence Johnston's planting was entirely original. It was the very opposite of the conventional herbaceous border setting, so popular among his contemporaries. His blending of sophistication and simplicity was unique. Nowhere else, except perhaps at [the later] Sissinghurst, are unusual plants found growing in cottage garden-like settings. This conception of little gardens within a large garden was entirely novel, as were the tapestry hedges and many other schemes.[1]

When the First World War broke out, Johnston was forty-three. He nevertheless went to the Western Front as a member of the British Expeditionary Force, as a major in the hussars. Wounded and left for dead, he was fortunate that the officer of a burial party saw him move and recognised him. Having recovered from his wounds, he returned to the front in 1916, serving with the Northumberland Regiment, from which he only retired in 1922. He then returned to Hidcote, where the garden had been neglected during his absence, and for the first time employed a head gardener in the person of Frank Adams. For both men, gardening was a consuming passion, evening after evening being spent planning new projects – somewhat to the annoyance of Mrs Adams. After Mrs Winthrop's death in 1926, Johnston's delight in plants led him to hunt for new species in South America, South Africa and the Far East.

The garden became famous. It delighted Mary Anderson's Italian friends when she took them there, as well as many other visitors. Johnston acquired a wide circle

of gardening friends, including the garden designer Norah Lindsay, and he was a prominent member of the Royal Horticultural Society and a member of the elite Garden Club. But not even his experience in the army, where he must have had to get on with a wide section of humanity, made him clubbable. Adopting the outward appearance of a country gentleman, wearing the plus fours so popular in that era, he remained an enigma whose greatest act of self-expression was Hidcote.

After the Second World War, Johnston went to live, for the sake of his health, at La Serre de la Madone, behind Menton in the south of France, entrusting Hidcote to Mrs Lindsay. After her sudden death in 1948, Vita Sackville-West and others persuaded the National Trust to acquire Hidcote Manor for the nation, on the basis of its horticultural merit.

'Would it be misleading to call Hidcote a cottage garden on the most glorified scale?' asked Sackville-West.[2] Because of the National Trust's careful stewardship, visitors to Hidcote can decide the point for themselves, as they stroll past the hydrangeas of the forecourt, emerge into the long walk, look towards the two little Cotswold stone summer houses or pavilions with their upsweeping roofs, enjoy the view through the wrought-iron grille of the gates, delight in the old-fashioned roses, explore the dozens of separate little gardens enclosed by hedges, and wander amid the several acres of shrubs and trees that form the Wilderness.

Like Gertrude Jekyll's, Johnston's approach to design was essentially painterly. The White Garden, which was originally planted with summer phlox, predates that at Sissinghurst. As adherents of the Arts and Crafts movement, Jekyll and Johnston were conscious of the old traditions that were disappearing from rural England. In this way the garden became a hymn to Johnston's adopted country, expressed with the horticultural subtlety of a connoisseur. His mother, although American, had brought him up to love the arts and culture of the Old World, and in Hidcote he made his own contribution to the European tradition.

When Johnston himself died in 1958, he was buried in the churchyard at Mickleton, near Hidcote Manor, beside his mother.

ABOVE An old cedar of Lebanon was one of the few garden features at Hidcote before Johnston began work.

MAUD
CUNARD

AT

NEVILL HOLT

Few people can have thought that Sir Bache Cunard, Baronet, and Maud Alice Burke made the perfect couple. Cunard's sister certainly did not: she attempted to persuade Maud to abandon the marriage, but Maud was sure of her own mind. For a lively young woman, expected to observe the social proprieties of the age, marriage was a passport to greater personal freedom. This one, made in New York, would also give her a position in England, where, in due course, she took London by storm.

PREVIOUS PAGES The mid-fifteenth century oriel window is the glory of Nevill Holt, Leicestershire: reminiscent of Crosby Hall in London, the sumptuous town house of a merchant, built after 1466, but decoratively finer. The roof bosses are exceptionally fine. In this photograph, the 'olden time' mood is enriched by armour and pikes, oak furniture, moose heads and an enormous Chinese bronze jardinière.

Sir Bache and Lady Cunard in Hyde Park, 1915. The couple had separated four years before.

In 1894 Bache was forty-three and no longer the sharply dressed blade caricatured in the Spy cartoon which appeared in *Vanity Fair* thirteen years earlier. Heavily set, his melancholy air was not improved by a down-turning moustache that might have been a furry animal – not, though, a fox. For this grandson of the founder of the famous Cunard Line, Bache, although born in New York, had made fox-hunting his main occupation. At the age of twenty-seven he had bought a pack of hounds in Leicestershire; he was 'deservedly popular', according to *Baily's Monthly Magazine of Sports and Pastimes*. Although already 'not a light weight', he rode 'boldly to hounds on very good horses'. Previously, he was 'wonderfully quick and very keen' at polo but stopped after his brother, Edward, was killed playing it. Shortly before he died, Edward had bought Nevill Holt, an ancient place in one of the best hunting countries in England. Sir Bache inherited both the house and the baronetcy from his brother. He shot, he drove carriages four-in-hand, and liked to craft ingenious trinkets out of metal and carved coconut shells. It was to Nevill Holt that he brought his bride.

Maud was blue-eyed, sparky and twenty-three. Although her family was rich, the money came from California, then a socially unknown land where she had, nonetheless, already acquired 'a past'. Her mother was attractive to men and there was some question as to whether her father had really been James Burke, who died when she was a girl. Afterwards, Horace Carpentier, who had been a general in the American Civil War,

became an intimate of the household. Carpentier, a cultivated bibliophile, also liked collecting young girls, whom he called his 'nieces', likened to 'first editions, in mint condition, with leaves uncut'.[1] Maud Burke became niece-in-chief. Uncle Horace encouraged a love of poetry, Shakespeare and novel reading (Maud's favourite in English being, rather surprisingly, Samuel Richardson's Pamela, with its agonisingly virtuous young heroine), as well as music. He took Maud, aged twelve, to hear the *Ring Cycle* at the Metropolitan Opera in New York, to which she responded with rapture. She played the piano. Maud's mother took her travelling in Europe, and there she met another man, who, like Sir Bache and Carpentier, was some decades older than her: the writer George Moore, a freethinker who, as part of the Celtic Revival, would sometimes disappear into Ireland, but otherwise rejoiced in his position of literary lion in and around London. She met him at a big luncheon at the Savoy, slipping into the dining room before the event to switch the place cards in order to ensure that she sat next to him. Moore idolised her free if somewhat skittish spirit, and she became his muse and lover. The marriage to Bache had been precipitated by a disaster in San Francisco, when – lacking the *savoir-faire* of a May Goelet – she overplayed her hand with Prince André Poniatowski, to the extent that the press announced their engagement. Somewhat caddishly, Poniatowski insisted on a public recantation. She escaped to New York, met Bache and perhaps married him to get away from the fuss. Her marriage would never provide more than an intermezzo in a non-exclusive relationship with Moore that lasted forty years.

To a sportsman such as Bache, Nevill Holt was remarkable principally for its views: situated on the crest of a hill, it looks out over a Midlands landscape of hedges and copses, with Rockingham Castle just visible on the horizon. That could only mean foxes

> To a sportsman such as Bache, Nevill Holt was remarkable principally for its views: situated on the crest of a hill, it looks out over a Midlands landscape of hedges and copses, with Rockingham Castle just visible on the horizon. That could only mean foxes and, where the latter permitted, pheasants.

RIGHT The Irish novelist George Moore in about 1880. With the conductor Sir Thomas Beecham, he was one of Lady Cunard's most attentive admirers.

OPPOSITE The great hall at Nevill Holt, decorated in baronial taste with armour and oak furniture. Lady Cunard believed that oak was appropriate to the style of the house, although she loved to introduce sensuous textiles and colour.

Cliché Bulloz.

ÉDOUARD MANET
Le romancier George Moore, esquisse.

and, where the latter permitted, pheasants. Architecturally, it looks like a game of consequences, where every century since the thirteenth has contributed part of the story – generally adding a portion but rarely making sense of the whole. The Nevills had found themselves on the wrong side during the English Civil War and afterwards remained Roman Catholics. As a result, they did not have the money to tidy the house up during the Georgian period. This would probably have been a plus to the Victorian Bache: Old English houses were in vogue; so was hunting.

Fox-hunting had begun as a fashionable pastime in eighteenth-century Sussex, where lighter soil allowed horses to gallop faster. But improved drainage allowed Leicestershire and Northamptonshire to develop into the 'cut-me-down countries' of which Mr Jorrocks stood in awe. Bullocks which had been driven from Wales were fattened on old pasture, some of it ancient ridge and furrow, with stout hedges to keep them in. This combination of features ensured that the districts around Melton Mowbray and Market Harborough remained fashionable with what Matthew Arnold would have called the Philistines for more than a century. Nevill Holt was centrally located in hunting's Mecca.

Clearly, Sir Bache, if not his wife, needed a house that would be equal to the demands of late Victorian house parties throughout the hunting season. The ancient great hall was made more convincingly Gothic, a new range with a bay window inspired by the Gothic oriel was added next to the church and quantities of dark panelling were introduced to many rooms in the house. Naturally the stables had to be extended: ten grooms were living at Nevill Holt, according to the 1881 census. But the money could not keep up with the lifestyle: a reason, perhaps, for Bache's late marriage.

It was not long before G. M., as George Moore was invariably known, was a regular visitor at Nevill Holt, at first while Bache was away on fishing trips, later openly. Maud's daughter Nancy, poet and political activist, was rumoured to be his daughter.

Uninterested in outdoor pursuits, Maud found solace in decoration. She expelled the Victorian furniture and replaced it with oak that suited the architecture. Rooms were rearranged to bring out the sensuous qualities of the silk and satin fabrics, and the rich colours of the rugs. Nancy remembered her mother's 'genius for beautifying ... creating, transforming, humanising'.[2] Bache made a garden gate, typically out of horseshoes for

LEFT Emerald Cunard (as she had become, having changed her name from Maud) attends the Strauss Ball at the Savoy Hotel, with the Maharajah of Alwar, January 7, 1931.

OPPOSITE Cecil Beaton's portrait of Emerald Cunard shows something of the wit and vivacity which drew artists, politicians, authors, socialites and royalty to her salons. 'It was impossible to be bored in her house,' recalled Harold Acton.

Appropriately, 20 Cavendish Square was decorated in the vivid manner of the Ballet Russe which was then in vogue: it was a stage set.

ponies, to tempt her, like her Tennysonian namesake, to 'come into the garden'; the gambit was a failure. Particularly when her husband was away, she filled the house with a witty and artistic set, who were separated from Bache's hunting friends by a barrier of mutual incomprehension.

Nevill Holt was thought to be sufficiently smart to convey a 'social benediction', in the words of the society gossip writer Elsa Maxwell, on those who went there. But the tone of the house, under Maud's hand, was bohemian. The author Daphne Fielding (Marchioness of Bath during her first marriage), who was a friend of Nancy Cunard, described the scene:

Romantic intrigue was a not uncommon element of Maud's house parties. She enjoyed having beautiful and ardent women to stay, voluptuous figures in tea gowns designed by Poiret, Worth or Reville, wafting a faint breath of heliotrope from their

trailing draperies as they brushed by; while she herself, looking like a Gavarni drawing, 'filled the air with unpremeditated music' [a quotation from George Moore's Letters to Lady Cunard] as she came into the room.

One warm August night a guest threw open the bedroom window and emitted the cry of the Valkyries. This elicited other Wagnerian responses from other windows. This night music became a nocturnal ritual for as long as the heat wave lasted. Maud described Bache's response when he returned from a fishing trip: 'He noticed an atmosphere of love. "I don't understand what is going on in this house," he said, "but I don't like it."'[3] The marriage ended. The money tap at Nevill Holt was turned off and, in 1914, it was sold.

In 1911 Maud decamped to London, first taking a relatively small house owned by the Prime Minister, H. H. Asquith, at 20 Cavendish Street, then moving to grander premises in Carlton House Terrace, before establishing herself in Grosvenor Square. These homes formed the backdrop to her salon. While French artists and littérateurs met aristocrats and bankers in the drawing rooms of Paris, London, at the end of the Edwardian decade, was a stuffier place. As often as not, sparkling conversation fell on ears that were deaf to its brilliance. Maud entertained on a new principle: she mixed the most amusing people she could find, from all areas of activity. Artists, scholars, poets, journalists, explorers, scholars and literary figures met aristocrats and members of the royal family. The polished young musician and future conductor Thomas Beecham, whose family manufactured the eponymous liver pills, had entered the lists against G. M. as Maud's constant inamorato, a role that, in the end, the two men shared. (This yielded a philanthropic benefit to English music, since Beecham enrolled Maud's chequebook and fundraising powers in his campaign to improve it.) Many of the habitués were rich. What mattered, though, was that they could talk. She introduced unlikely people to one another, generally with a preposterous résumé of their talents; she shook them up further through her own aperçus, which had the appearance of being the first thing that came into her mind. Daphne Fielding summed up the impression it made on her as a debutante: 'The young men I met at her house were far more entertaining than any of the Guards officers, budding stockbrokers and sporting characters who had hitherto been my lot at debutante dances and hunt balls.' Appropriately, 20 Cavendish Square was decorated in the vivid manner of the Ballet Russe which was then in vogue: it was a stage set.

Maud's reinvention was complete when, to the surprise even of her intimates, she changed her Christian name to Emerald. (She wore emeralds and was nicknamed the Emerald Queen, so she rather fancied it.) With investments in the United States, Emerald's finances were badly hit by the Wall Street Crash, but she soldiered on, with diminishing resources, through the Second World War until her death in 1948, by which time she was living in the Dorchester Hotel. Her eulogy can be found in *Memoirs of an Aesthete* by Harold Acton, the writer, scholar and dilettante who was a close friend:

> … we enjoyed an entrancing ballet of the hours. Her life was thoroughly spent not economised. Lady Cunard had created an ideal setting for a synthesis of the arts. One could only abandon oneself joyfully, inhaling the luxuriance of sight and sound until one was lapped into silence. The pretentiousness that paraded in other 'literary' houses was absent: there was never a false note.[4]

Bache had died in 1925, having lived alone at the Haycock Inn for eleven years. Mentally troubled, impoverished and an alcoholic, Nancy's end came in Paris, where she collapsed in 1965, weighing only sixty pounds.

By that stage, Nevill Holt had long been a prep school, having been bought in 1928 by a Englishman, Frederick Phillips, who, according to one of his sons, quoted in the *Times Educational Supplement*, claimed to be a French aristocrat with military honours.[5] The school closed in 1998. Its condition and outlook appeared bleak, but since 2000 it has undergone a renaissance as the home of David Ross, one of the founders of Carphone Warehouse.

GORDON SELFRIDGE

AND

HENGISTBURY HEAD

'A nd so nearly realised,' lamented the architect Philip Tilden of the castle that Gordon Selfridge almost built at Hengistbury Head, a wild headland on the Dorset coast. To Tilden, as to many people, Selfridge seemed little short of a force of nature. He had been brought up in Michigan. His father had a small retail business and his mother was a teacher. Becoming a bank clerk, he was unable to join the navy because of his size; but the direction of his career was made manifest when he joined the Chicago store that later became Marshall Field & Co. He would be a shopkeeper, like his father, but a great one.

PREVIOUS PAGES The American businessman Harry Gordon Selfridge, in uncharacteristically scholarly pose, photographed soon after the Selfridge department store had opened in 1909.

One of the perspectives that evokes the impossibly vast castle that Philip Tilden designed for Selfridge from 1919: a fantastic vision of dizzying grandeur and elegant romance.

As a rising talent at Marshall Field, Selfridge travelled widely, not least to Europe, but he could not persuade Marshall Field himself to establish a shop in London, and so left to set up on his own. In 1909, he succeeded in opening his own store on Oxford Street. London had seen nothing like it. Although executed by a local architect, R. F. Atkinson, the façade of swaggering giant columns had been designed by Chicago's Daniel Burnham, with a Beaux Arts bravura which expressed the spirit of the whole enterprise. When designing an 'S' that would form the store's logo, Selfridge did so using the symbols of the £ and $.[1]

The years 1890 to 1914 were the golden age of the London department store; the period during which the biggest and most flamboyant, Harrods among them, reached their zenith. But many of the great names had been around for a couple of generations, growing, like the mustard tree, from small beginnings. Benjamin Harvey started business in Knightsbridge in 1813, his daughter taking a silk buyer called Colonel Nichols into partnership, hence Harvey Nichols; Debenhams began the same year; Dickins & Jones (1790) and John Lewis (1864) were also long established, as was Whiteley's – although its founder, William Whiteley, had only died, from the bullet of a man claiming to be his son, in 1907. Selfridges had no such pedigree. It was new, and proud of it.

ABOVE Beaux-Arts bravura on Oxford Street: the Selfridge department store, opened in 1909. Selfridge did not trust an English architect to achieve the correct level of swaggering self-confidence: the design was provided by Daniel Burnham of Chicago.

LEFT Gordon Selfridge, around 1910, in his office in the department store, 'where telephones tinkled and demure young ladies brought in scraps of paper'.

Advertising and publicity were in their infancy, and Gordon Selfridge's ideas were considerably in advance of his British rivals'. He hired the best graphic designers to produce posters and brought over Marshall Field's chief window dresser from Chicago to glamorise the shopfront. Twelve hundred people worked in the store. They were not there only to sell. In addition, Selfridge offered a 'Library and Silence Room', where customers could refresh their minds and spirits away from the bustle of the street; also a bureau de change, a post office, a savings bank, booking offices for railway, steamship and theatre, a luncheon hall and a tea garden. It functioned as a kind of club for the sophisticated shopper; the public loved it. (Had Selfridge perhaps borrowed the club idea from Harrods, which had actual clubs for gentlemen and ladies – to join, apply to the secretary?)

Selfridge: That was what people called him. The surname was enough – no Christian name, no initial, not even a Mr. In the manner of an impresario, he fed the myth, living up entirely to public expectation, not least in where he chose to live. From the Marquess of Lansdowne he rented Lansdowne's House, situated between Berkeley Square and Piccadilly, designed by Robert Adam for the politician who negotiated the peace with America that ended the American Revolutionary War, and Highcliffe Castle, overlooking Christchurch Bay in Hampshire. Selfridge liked some things about Highcliffe: the

ABOVE Highcliffe Castle, on the Hampshire coast, built in the 1830s. When Selfridge rented it as a country house, he was pleased by the thought that it had previously received the Kaiser.

fact that it had, for example, housed the Kaiser for three and a half weeks in 1907. As a castle, though, it was unsatisfactory, having been built only in the 1830s for Lord Stuart de Rothesay – a romantic, as may be surmised from his name, the 'de Rothesay' being a mere embellishment. Although parts of the castle had been brought from ruins in Normandy, the general effect was one of picturesque caprice rather than antique aggression, and to some of Selfridge's colleagues the effect of Gothic arches and stained glass was 'churchy': they felt bound to lower their voices when among them.[2]

Selfridge ate copiously, smoked a couple of cigars a day, exercised little but drank nothing stronger than water. Abstention from alcohol did nothing to dent his desire to entertain, an urge not quashed by the death of his wife in 1918. Thereafter, his elderly mother, 'a hostesses of the rare old school of American propriety, lavender, lace, and an exquisite link with old standards', presided over parties that were largely decorous (the worst episode that one Selfridge's director, A. H. Williams, remembered seeing was a drunkard on the dance floor lurching into a rare Cretan terracotta statue which smashed on the floor. 'The tipsy guest surveyed the debris of a moment and then began to kick the pieces off the floor. Selfridge watched him with a mask-like face in silence.') But urges of another kind also overtook him. As he entered old age, he lavished money on young women, among them Jenny Dolly of Vaudeville performers the Dolly Sisters. His behaviour while cavorting in France was not as decorous as his mother, living in England, might have

wished, and he gambled heavily. The store was not big enough to support such a lifestyle, but, with boundless optimism, Selfridge saw no reason to rein in. And Tilden, encouraged by Selfridge, let his imagination soar. He drew up the plan and design of his castle on a specially small scale, that being the only way he could fit it on to a single sheet of paper.

'You know, Philip, Selfridge is going to build a castle,' Martin Conway, the explorer and art historian had told him in 1919. The sadness of having recently lost his wife had clearly not blunted Selfridge's ambition; perhaps the immediate awareness of mortality had merely quickened it. Tilden met the great retailer over lunch at the Ritz, an event followed by many other lunches in Selfridge's office at the department store, 'where telephones tinkled and demure young ladies brought in scraps of paper'. Site visits followed:

> We used to motor to the swift channel that disgorges the rushing water of the Christchurch Avon into the sea, then, after crossing tipsily, and plodding along difficult tracks, mount to the highest point of this peninsula. There was a magnificent outlook, for upon clear days we could see the Isle of Wight, crenellated in its chalkiness, the isolated Needles standing gaunt and apart, the blue Channel with its passing liners lying untroubled to the horizon, and inland, the country besmeared with the modern red roofs of a teeming and pervading Bournemouth, gradually losing itself in the haze of woodland round Kingston Lacy, Fordingbridge and Wimborne.

Here, on this commanding spot, Selfridge intended to build his castle.[3] Selfridge was a man of strong instinct: it had made the success of his firm. But he had no sense of humour to puncture the balloon of his self-belief, or steer him away from pomposity. 'I have bought a part of England, Williams,' he told his publicity direct proudly, after the purchase of Hengistbury Head had gone through.

'I have always tried to build well,' he said. 'I have left my mark on London for a long time to come. But Hengistbury will be my own.'

As he rolled up the drawings, he turned to me and said in a low voice, as if he were imparting a confidence:

'I love England, Williams.'

To Williams, the theatricality of the declaration seemed laughable, but for a man who rarely revealed his inner feelings it said much.

Although Selfridges in Oxford Street, had been assertively classical, Gordon Selfridge believed that Gothic was England's national style. Tilden found this characteristically American. He had already been 'amazed' at the emotion shown by people from the United States when standing in front of Gothic buildings,

> Not in the least differentiating, as far as I could see, between buildings of the mightiest of Gothic periods, and those produced during the pseudo-Gothic phases: the Walpole Gothic of the eighteenth century – that which was fostered by Gray's Elegy and all that it stood for in the way of church towers, ruins, owls and ivy – the Walter Scott Gothic, revived romantically through the influence of the Waverley novels, and that of Pugin, leading to the Gothic of the nineteenth-century pundits, partially under the influence of Ruskin.

To an experienced practitioner such as Tilden, who, like any aesthetically inclined European, had grown up surrounded by the works of the distant past, the distinctions of style and period were more obvious than they were to a neophyte such as Selfridge. What he lacked in subtlety of appreciation, however, he made up for with his certainty of conviction. Gothic may have been the national style, but English architecture had got it all wrong. Too much of it was – having perhaps been built in different ages – unsymmetrical and out of balance. What was needed was Gothic on a regular classical plan.

What [Selfridge] lacked in subtlety of appreciation, however, he made up for with his certainty of conviction. Gothic may have been the national style, but English architecture had got it all wrong.

THESE PAGES Philip Tilden's designs for Selfridge's megalomaniac Hengistbury Head. Selfridge had been struck by the unfailing appeal, particularly to Americans, of great Gothic buildings, but felt they would be improved by greater scale and regularity. Between them, architect and client evolved a project for a truly titanic palace, with two drives sweeping up to a gate that would ultimately lead to three entrances: one giving access to theatre, picture galleries, tennis courts, baths; one to the heart of the building; and one to the great hall. 'The plan of the house,' recalled Tilden, 'was immense.'

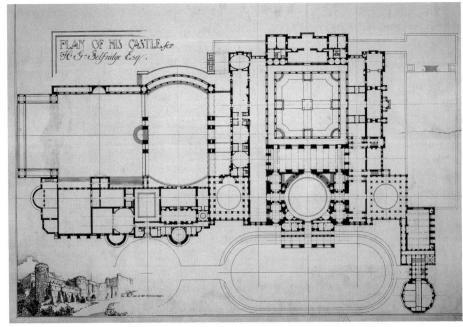

The castle that Selfridge and Tilden evolved in their minds was titanic. 'The plan of the house was immense.' Two drives swept up from the flat land through a gate like that into a Spanish city. They continued, twining over each other, but finally separating, the upper one rising into a kind of piazza. Here were three entrances, leading to the theatre, picture galleries, tennis courts and baths; secondly, to the heart of the building; and thirdly to a great hall attached to a tower so huge that it would dominate the landscape as far as the eye could see. The whole plan was strung on one great vista, more than 1,000 feet long, and widening centrally at the main entrance.

Perhaps one should be thankful that their vision was never realised. Tilden thought that readers might consider the descriptions in his autobiography to be 'like some exuberant catalogue of the dreams of an eastern visionary palace', the effect of which would be cloyingly over-rich. Those today might feel that it bears a sinister similarity to work that would be carried in another European country in the next decade by Albert Speer.

It was not to be. Selfridge found that the income he could draw from his business barely covered the outgoings of his existing lifestyle, in two expensively rented houses, let alone the construction of a castle-palace on a scale to challenge Versailles. When Selfridge's mother died, the pace of dissipation accelerated. In 1947, he himself died in a rented flat on Putney Heath where he lived with one of his three children. His fortune had gone. He was buried in the churchyard at Highcliffe beside his mother and his wife.

NANCY LANCASTER

AT

KELMARSH HALL,
DITCHLEY PARK &
HASELEY COURT

In the 1920s, Nancy Lancaster, née Perkins, had been reluctant to make her life in England. By the end of the century, this had come to seem a distinct irony, because her eye for interesting furniture and faded textiles, combined with an American sense of comfort, created a look that set the style of the English country house for a generation.

PREVIOUS PAGES The Velvet Room at Ditchley Park. Nancy Lancaster did more than anyone to establish the classic 'country-house look' of the mid-twentieth century.

Nancy Lancaster dressed for the 1935 Silver Jubilee Ball at Buckingham Palace. The Astor tiara was borrowed from her Aunt Nancy, Lady Astor, with its famous Sancy diamond.

RIGHT Brought up in Virginia, Nancy was a superb horsewoman. Schooling a young horse in 1924, she fell badly. It was after her husband Ronald Tree had nursed her back to health that she agreed to move to England.

OPPOSITE The Pytchley Hunt was one of the smartest packs between the Wars. Both the Prince of Wales (future Edward VIII) and Duke of York (future George VI) hunted with it, and it had not forgotten the beautiful Empress of Austria, who caused a flutter in many hearts when riding to hounds in the Victorian period.

Born in 1897 and brought up in Albemarle County, Virginia, where her father owned a not particularly successful meat-packing business, Nancy's first husband had been Henry Field, a grandson of Marshall Field of the eponymous Chicago store. Cole Porter was an usher at the wedding. Tragically, what should have been a routine operation to remove Henry Field's tonsils gave him blood poisoning, and he died at the age of only twenty-two. Nancy was now a rich widow. Crossing the Atlantic by liner, she met Field's cousin, Ronald Tree. They shared, among other things, a passion for horses, and were married in London in 1920. Nancy was too attached to her childhood summer home of Mirador, a brick Virginian mansion of the 1830s, which she tactfully remodelled and decorated, to think of making her principal home overseas.

Ronnie, however, was an Anglophile and did not see a future for himself in American public life. In 1924, Nancy had a bad fall while schooling a young horse, after which Ronnie nursed her back to health. She repaid his devotion by agreeing to move to England. They settled in Northamptonshire where, in 1926, Ronnie was offered the joint mastership of the prestigious Pytchley Hunt. This crème de la crème of fox hunts – riding over ancient ridge and furrow pasture that had not been disturbed since the Middle Ages

and jumping the formidable hedges that were required to keep bullocks being fattened on the grass from roaming – attracted the attention of the royal family itself. This gave Ronnie a position of influence in the shires, which he extended, seven years later, by becoming an MP. As their country house, the Trees took a lease on Kelmarsh Hall.

Mirador had already introduced Nancy to the joys of reviving old houses. There, her mentor had been the architect William Delano, whose work showed how a loved but poorly proportioned plantation house could be transformed into a place of classical elegance, without dispelling the sacred family memories that it enshrined. A top-lit rotunda was created in the centre of the house, and behind, views of the Blue Ridge Mountains were framed by a pergola, over which wisteria twined: to Delano, the garden was the natural extension of the house.[1] Meanwhile, for their New York house, the Trees leased 7 East 96th Street from the gentleman decorator Ogden Codman, who had co-written *The Decoration of Houses* with the writer Edith Wharton. Codman's cool and reticent classicism would be absorbed as an ingredient of Nancy's own style, as it evolved at Kelmarsh Hall.

Kelmarsh, however, was on a grander scale than Mirador, having been designed in the 1720s by James Gibbs. A Catholic Scot who had studied in Rome, Gibbs leant towards the baroque in his churches and public buildings, but at Kelmarsh produced a restrained essay in English Palladianism, with a pedimented centre block linked to

If Nancy felt intimidated by the prospect of such a house, her confidence would have been strengthened by the example of her aunt, Nancy Astor, at Cliveden, whose wit, energy and outspokenness she shared.

pavilions by quadrants. If Nancy felt intimidated by the prospect of such a house, her confidence would have been strengthened by the example of her aunt, Nancy Astor, at Cliveden, whose wit, energy and outspokenness she shared. She also had an uncle by marriage who was an architect, the Hon. Paul Phipps; the 'fascinating'[2] Phipps was a pupil of Lutyens, who had married Nancy Astor's sister, Nora Langhorne (for whom he did not, alas, prove fascinating enough: she left him after giving birth to two children, one of whom was the future entertainer Joyce Grenfell). Phipps, who built a number of houses in partnership with another Lutyens pupil, Oswald P. Milne, installed central heating, electric lighting and proper bathrooms. The last was an undoubted novelty in Britain. In Nancy's words:

> People would rush to the lavatory or rush to the bathroom to get ahead of the line. Even at a big house like Cliveden there were only two baths to a floor. You'd see breadlines outside the doors, with people in their dressing gowns, carrying their sponge bags, waiting for a bath.[3]

This was not Nancy's style. Downstairs, the Victorian ballroom was turned into a dining room, for the big house parties which the master of the Pytchley entertained. It was furnished with Chippendale chairs upholstered in dandelion-yellow leather. The library was given panelling, the design of which was entrusted not to Phipps but to Delano; and altogether Nancy delighted in the shabbiness she found at Kelmarsh – it reminded her of some Virginian homes – the decoration of the hall, painted a dreary green and hung with armour, needed refreshing. Phipps introduced Nancy to a paint specialist called Mr Kick, who had an artist's appreciation of how light plays in a room.

OPPOSITE Kelmarsh Hall, Northamptonshire, built in 1727–32 by James Gibbs. Nancy Lancaster and her first husband Ronnie Tree took a lease on the house in 1926, to hunt with the Pytchley. She returned to it after having married Kelmarsh's owner Major Claude Lancaster in 1948.

ABOVE The Chinese room at Kelmarsh, which Mrs Lancaster regarded as the prettiest in the house. She hung it with old Chinese wallpaper taken from Kimberley Hall in Norfolk, along with the chimneypiece.

RIGHT The west front of Ditchley Park, Oxfordshire. Built by Francis Smith to the designs of James Gibbs for the 2nd Earl of Lichfield. Its bravura style appealed particularly to Nancy Lancaster's then husband Ronnie Tree.

In *Nancy Lancaster*, Martin Wood describes Nancy's desire to decorate the hall at Kelmarsh in the same colour as Lady Islington's dining room at Rushbrooke Hall, a Tudor mansion in Suffolk. Kick visited Rushbrooke and returned with two samples: 'One the colour that Nancy wanted and one almost the colour of brown paper'. The former would have looked like knicker elastic; the latter would appear to be the right colour under the changing light. Kick applied no fewer than eight coats of paint. He went on to work for Nancy over the next thirty years. In the 1950s, during Nancy's second spell at Kelmarsh, the hall was repainted under the direction of John Fowler. Sir Albert Richardson was also employed to remove the house's nineteenth-century accretions and return it to the purity of its eighteenth-century state.

Some of the money, if not the fun, went out of hunting in the Depression of the 1930s, but Ronnie and Nancy had found a new passion. Ronnie described their first exposure to Ditchley Park, in Oxfordshire, in his autobiography, *When the Moon Was High*. They emerged from a lane of hedges, entwined with honeysuckle and wild roses, into a double avenue of beech trees leading to the gate lodge. Before them was a heavily wooded park: 'We marvelled at it ... Ahead, another avenue of elm trees, and then the house itself appeared, stark grey against the blue sky, its two lead statues of Loyalty and Fame looking far out over the trees towards the Churchill palace at Blenheim, its neighbour to the east.' The previous owner, Lord Dillon, had recently died, and they were met by an old butler in a red wig. Some of Lord Dillon's relatives produced Champagne. Ronnie had bought the house within a fortnight.

Ditchley was built by Francis Smith to a design, again, by Gibbs. But it was bigger and more magnificent: the roof is hidden by a parapet, on which stand urns and statues, and the hall is ornamented with plasterwork. This did not entirely suit Nancy's domestic ideal – she thought it might be difficult to live in. Until her own modernising hand had passed over it, she and her husband were preceded to their sleeping quarters by the butler, carrying an acetylene lamp. She again called on Phipps to overcome the deficiencies in heating, lighting and plumbing, while summoning the luminaries of the decorating world – Lady Colefax, Syrie Maugham, and Stéphane Boudin of Paris – to advise on aspects of the interior. But the controlling taste that made a synthesis of these different contributions belonged to the Trees. Their son Michael later observed that 'my parents, from a decorating point of view, were a marvellous pair'.

Ronnie's department was the purchase of furniture, appropriate to the baroque richness of the rooms. It was Nancy who composed the rooms and chose the silks, velvets, damasks and brocades, leaving them unfurled about the house so that gaudy colours would be bleached by the sun. In the hall, she took a penknife to the battleship-grey paintwork, scraping back to the original grey-blue or dove-grey of the eighteenth-century scheme – an early if primitive example of a paint scrape to research the decorative history of a room. To this she added red upholstery, in a note derived from a portrait of Ditchley's builder, Lord Lichfield, over the fireplace. When work was finished, the Trees commissioned the Russian artist Alexandre Serebriakoff to paint a series of watercolours of the achievement, showing a house that is as balanced and calm, yet vivacious, as a Haydn symphony.

Nancy was not afraid of rich colours and bold patterns, accompanied, as in the Velvet Room, by an equally bold carpet – in a room whose architecture is itself opulent and gilded. The velvet had been bought by Lord Lichfield's brother, Admiral Fitzroy Lee, in Genoa when he was commander of the Mediterranean Fleet. While any one piece of exuberance would have drawn attention to itself, the effect of such a concentration of incident created a feeling of voluptuous repose. Nancy recalled that the room was used every night: 'England is so cold in the winter, but that room was the warmest in the world. It was cozy, but I have to say I never liked the velvet.'[4]

Nancy's success was acknowledged, and she was asked to help other owners with their houses. Outside, the terrace of the garden was restored from plans found in Sir John Soane's Museum at Lincoln's Inn Fields in London. Pheasant and partridge shooting replaced hunting as the sport of choice, and

Nancy was not afraid of rich colours and bold patterns, accompanied, as in the Velvet Room, by an equally bold carpet – in a room whose architecture is itself opulent and gilded.

ABOVE Alexandre Serebriakoff's
painting of the hall at Ditchley.
Order and comfort characterised
Nancy Lancaster's interiors, in
contrast to the exuberant but
under-heated condition of many
country houses in the earlier
twentieth century.

ABOVE The white drawing room at
Ditchley Park, decorated with the
grand simplicity that was Nancy
Lancaster's hallmark. The house was
designed in 1722 by James Gibbs.

OPPOSITE Nancy Lancaster at Haseley Court, Oxfordshire, by Cecil Beaton. Despite the air of control that she exudes in this photograph, tempers were frayed during the decoration of Haseley: she argued constantly with her collaborator John Fowler, and constantly changed her mind. Decorative harmony was, however, the result.

BELOW Nancy Lancaster considered 150 houses before buying her last home, Haseley Court in Oxfordshire, in 1954. She called it 'a lovely early Georgian house of silver stone', although it was in a poor state of repair, having been used as a prisoner-of-war camp.

Nancy – unusually for the time – took her place in the line of guns. On Saturday nights, thirty people would sit down to dinner, politicians and aristocrats like Anthony Eden and Lord Cranborne (later 5th Marquess of Salisbury) rubbing shoulders with such musical celebrities and film stars as Noël Coward and David Niven. A thousand guests, wearing red and white, came to the house-warming – 'the best party anybody has seen for many years', according to *Vogue* – in 1937.

The formality of the entertaining, like the decor, was laced with originality and Nancy's own lightness of touch, which made it, for the younger set, 'a bit more fun' than Cliveden and other country houses.[5] During the Second World War, hospitality went into a different gear, since Ditchley was considered to be a safer weekend destination for Winston Churchill than the Prime Minister's official residence at Chequers, when a full moon made the latter a clear target for enemy bombers. (Nancy Astor, who loved to tease Churchill just as much as he baited her, was not invited.)

Nancy contributed to the war effort by establishing a fleet of mobile canteens to take food to bombed towns and cities, including Coventry. With both her sons in the British Army, she not only changed her citizenship but brought her money to Britain in 1944 – with disastrous consequences to her finances.

The Trees' marriage did not long survive the war and they divorced in 1947. The next year, Nancy married for the third time, her new husband being Major Claude ('Juby') Lancaster, the owner of Kelmarsh Hall. Perhaps, as her children believed, she loved Kelmarsh more than Lancaster, because that marriage foundered after three years. But until her death in 1994 she remained Nancy Lancaster, a name that became synonymous with faultless taste in decoration.

LEFT The south wall of the saloon at Haseley Court. Reflected in the neo-Classical pier glasses are a pair of early seventeenth century portraits of Anne and Mary Fitton in white dresses (Mary may have been the Dark Lady of Shakespeare's Sonnets) which had hung at Ditchley. The walls were lined with aquamarine silk.

RIGHT Cecil Beaton's photo of Nancy in the hall of Haseley. Her intention was that the house should be 'light and bright,' with an air of 'studied carelessness'.

Ronnie having bought her Sibyl Colefax's share of the decorating firm Colefax & Fowler, she lent her impeccable eye to the arrangement of many of Britain's most delightful country houses and gardens, including such palatial examples as Boughton House and Badminton Park. Fowler, as Hugo Vickers has described, was 'the perfect foil for her. He was the observant outsider, an expert on the eighteenth century, and an artist, reviving stippling and dragging, while she preferred the overall look, applying her yardstick of elegance and comfort.'[6]

A thousand guests, wearing red and white, came to the house-warming – 'the best party anybody has seen for many years', according to *Vogue* – in 1937.

Nancy had considered 150 houses before buying her last home, Haseley Court in Oxfordshire, in 1954. 'I happen to like houses that remind me of Virginia,' she recalled. Run down after the use as a prisoner-of-war camp, Haseley was nevertheless 'a lovely early Georgian house of silver stone', and if rabbits scuttled through the self-seeded daisies, it possessed 'a view of the Chiltern Hills that reminded me of a miniature Blue Ridge Mountains'. Nancy loved the house back to life, although 'it would have been cheaper if I'd bought Versailles'. She copied the wallpaper for the Palladian Room from one at Drottningholm Palace in Sweden, after a sketch made for her by the King of Sweden himself.

WILLIAM RANDOLPH HEARST

AT

ST DONAT'S

At the end of a European tour, William Randolph Hearst was in London. 'Let's go down to St Donat's and look it over,' he suggested to members of his entourage.[1] The year was 1928 and he had bought the castle three years earlier but had not yet seen it. Hearst, in company with Marion Davies and other Hollywood friends, as well as his architect, Sir Charles Allom, knighted for his interior decoration of Buckingham Palace for George V, drove the 160 miles to Llantwit Major, on the north (Welsh) side of the Bristol Channel, arriving in the late afternoon. There followed a tour of the house and grounds, the inner stone recesses of the ancient structure being explored with the aid of kerosene lamps. The next morning, Hearst drove to Southampton to take a liner back to the United States and his newspaper empire. That one visit enabled him to dictate a twenty-five-page letter to Allom when he got there.

PREVIOUS PAGES The approach to the banqueting hall at St Donat's is made through a fifteenth-century Gothic screen imported from Devon.

William Randolph Hearst, 1863–1951: his sober appearance belies his energy, if not rapacity as both newspaper man and a collector.

The episode illustrates many aspects of Hearst's relationship with medieval architecture. He was greedy for it. He gobbled up old structures with a voracious appetite that barely left him time to digest his acquisitions. He had, though, an exceptional memory, and time and distance were to be annihilated in pursuit of his latest *bonne bouche*. Perched above precipitous cliffs, with gatehouse and battlements, St Donat's was a feast of grey stone and history. But its position in South Wales was hardly convenient for a man who was always in a hurry. That hardly mattered. In his lifetime, Hearst made no more than half a dozen visits to his property. It was a stage set, a pleasure dome, a dream in which Hearst could indulge himself from the other side of the Atlantic. He treated it, curiously, in much the same way that Henry VIII – another famously gluttonous autocrat – used his sixty-three palaces: for short, intense visits with his court, during which the place was full of life, being left to echo and perhaps moulder when the owner was not there. The difference was that, when the King was not present, Henry's palaces were empty shells: he brought his tapestries, furniture and plate with him. St Donat's was kept permanently dressed, sometimes in clothes that belonged elsewhere.

Hearst was already experienced in building. As early as 1891, a well head in Verona, north-east Italy, had caught his eye; he bought it, shipped the five tons of stones back to San Francisco and re-erected it there, before eventually transporting it to Mexico, where it gave the name to La Hacienda del Pozo de Verona. Since inheriting the 40,000-acre San Simeon in 1919, he had been employing Julia Hunt Morgan to transform the old camp into 'a little something' – which turned into a big Spanish baroque something of 165 rooms. Twelve years earlier, he had bid against J. D. Rockefeller Jr for stained-glass windows, weather vanes, Renaissance doorways, ancient sarcophagi, well heads and other objects from the architect Stanford White's collection, including a ceiling decorated with *Angels Bringing Tidings of Christ's Birth* which was later installed in the Doge's Suite at San Simeon.[2] Each day he would visit art galleries and auction houses and correspond with dealers all over Europe. He bought all kinds of objects, some conventionally portable, others not. Those in the latter category were used to enrich his various homes, including St Donat's.

His search for a castle began when he telegraphed Alice Head, managing director of his English subsidiary, the National Magazine Company: 'WANT BUY CASTLE IN ENGLAND'. William Waldorf Astor might have understood the impulse, but would have been appalled by the jumbling of ancient architectural body parts that took place at St Donat's – and horrified to think that his example might have inspired it. But so it was.

When Hearst considered acquiring Leeds Castle in Kent, Miss Head wrote to her chief that, given investment, it could 'be made quite as attractive as J. J. Astor [Astor's second son, John Jacob Astor V] has made Hever Castle'. Leeds, although it would have been convenient for London and Southampton, was rejected as being too primitive:

The episode illustrates many aspects of Hearst's relationship with medieval architecture. He was greedy for it. He gobbled up old structures with a voracious appetite that barely left him time to digest his acquisitions.

LEFT William Randolph Hearst and Marion Davies. Hearst's interference in Davies's career, after they had become lovers, did her reputation no favours.

FOLLOWING PAGES William Randolph Hearst's San Simeon in California. It reflects the newspaper tycoon's passion for architecture and entertaining, although the surfaces of poured concrete are less sympathetic than the Spanish Baroque architecture on which the structure is based. Taking the form of separate buildings grouped around highly architectural courtyards, its stationery bore the legend 'Hearst Camp': a reminder of its modest beginnings. Many of Hearst's purchases in Europe ended up here.

QUITE UNIQUE AS ANTIQUITY BUT NEEDS EXPENDITURE LARGE SUM TO MAKE IT HABITABLE NOT A BATH IN PLACE ONLY LIGHTING OIL LAMPS SERVANTS QUARTERS DOWN DUNGEONS AND IN STEEP BATTLEMENTED TOWERS STOP PART COULD BE MADE FIT TO LIVE IN BY SPENDING ABOUT FOUR THOUSAND.

It would be left to Lady Baillie to resolve the bathroom and lighting issues when she bought Leeds the next year. But when Miss Head visited St Donat's she was able to wire:

PERIOD PLACE IN EXCELLENT REPAIR WITH CENTRAL HEATING MODERN SANITATION STOP DONT WANT MISS IT.

Hearst did not miss it: the National Magazine Company bought it that October. 'This is our home,' says Orson Welles's character in *Citizen Kane*. The irony of that line, spoken to his dejected mistress, comes from the fact that 'home' was Xanadu,

In his lifetime, Hearst made no more than half a dozen visits to his property. It was a stage set, a pleasure dome, a dream in which Hearst could indulge himself from the other side of the Atlantic.

ABOVE The gatehouse and outer curtain wall were built in the late Middle Ages by the Stradline family who had acquired St Donat's through marriage in 1298.

RIGHT The de Hawey family built a stone case with a curtain wall in the late twelfth century. William Randolph Hearst employed Sir Charles Allom to turn it, quickly, into a luxurious mansion for occasion visits after he acquired it in 1925.

a megalomaniac's dream castle of gargantuan proportions. In the film, Kane stands at the foot of a sweeping marble staircase seemingly made for a colossus; the woman he addresses cowers beneath a French Gothic fireplace that is itself as big as a house. Charles Foster Kane was modelled on Hearst, Xanadu on San Simeon, the final resting place for many of the crate-loads of antique furniture that he had shipped over from Europe. St Donat's may not have been on that scale, but nowhere else does the romance of old materials for their own sake reach such a pitch of naked obsession. Romance, in fact, gave way to rape.

The tour that Hearst made of St Donat's in 1928 would have shown that the castle was in an exceptional state of repair. In the Victorian period it had been owned by the barrister and antiquarian Dr John Nicholl-Carne, who carried out two campaigns of works. After his death, it was purchased by the colliery owner Morgan Stuart Williams, who employed the great Gothic Revival partnership of Thomas Garner and G. F. Bodley to restore it thoroughly and add a large armoury for his collection of arms and armour. Photographs in *Country Life* show it to have been decorated in a spare but sensitive manner. Williams died in 1909, and St Donat's was eventually sold, in 1922, to the American diplomat Richard Pennoyer, who had married the Dowager Countess of Shrewsbury. The castle did not suit them and was sold to Hearst three years later, but after Williams's work, it was, as Head noted, in a sound structural condition.[3]

RIGHT The breakfast room. The fireplace came from the prior's lodging at Bradenstoke Priory, which was heavily quarried by Hearst. His depredations caused the Society for the Protection of Ancient Buildings to mount a public campaign.

ABOVE Hearst's armoury. What fun would there have been in a castle without the necessary trappings? Note the church brasses set into the sides of the arches.

Hearst's original twenty-five-page letter to Allom has been lost, but bathrooms would certainly have been mentioned. He needed sixty of them for house parties that might accommodate a hundred guests: their provision required a new water main to be laid from Bridgend. Electricity was also installed. Another topic must have been the acquisition of parts of old, preferably Gothic, buildings, because White Allom and other firms began supplying old chimneypieces the same year. During the 1920s, Hearst kept up an energetic correspondence with the loyal Miss Head. The subject was usually art or furniture sales and a communication such as the following, dated 8 February 1924, was not uncommon:

ARE THERE ANY IMPORTANT CEILINGS TO BE HAD IN ENGLAND ALSO STAIRCASES OF TUDOR OR JACOBEAN PERIOD WOULD LIKE ALSO ONE TRUSSED CEILING OF GUILD HALL TYPE HEARST.

Not all the purchases could be found a home. Many went to one of Hearst's two warehouses in the Bronx, New York. When, with new management trying to save the Hearst Corporation from financial ruin, these disgorged their treasures in 1937, one was found to hold 10,700 crates containing the stones of a Spanish monastery.

According to a National Magazine Company inventory of 1945 (entitled 'Mr W. R. Hearst's Property Insured as "Built In"'), Hearst had eighteen or so old chimneypieces or fireplaces moved to St Donat's. Most came from Acton Surgey Ltd or White Allom. They included a stone fireplace from Cadbury House, Yatton, as well as several fifteenth-century

He needed sixty of them [bathrooms] for house parties that might accommodate a hundred guests: their provision required a new water main to be laid from Bridgend.

ABOVE The recreation room at St Donat's, with billiard table beneath the heraldic banners. Hearst acquired St Donat's as a setting for parties during his brief visits to Britain. It was equipped with everything needed to amuse a cosmopolitan house party.

RIGHT The green bedroom, which was decorated for Hearst's mistress, the film star Marion Davies. It contained richly ornamented pieces of Anglo-Indian furniture.

chimneypieces, Gothic screens and minstrels' galleries, doorways and whole rooms. Not all fitted, so some had to be cut down, or else – in the case of one fireplace – the hood and frieze were supported on jambs from a different piece. The new banqueting hall created in the west range of the castle is reached through a fifteenth-century stone screen taken from a Devon church. In 1930 the elaborately carved and gilded ceiling was removed from St Botolph's, the famous parish church of Boston, Lincolnshire, known as Boston Stump: it had been found above the early nineteenth-century vault and sold, surreptitiously it seems, for just over £2,000 to pay for Sir Charles Nicholson's restoration of the church. The fireplace, with its tall hood (truncated by the comparatively low ceiling) and armorial shield of fleurs-de-lis, came from a château in Beauvais, northern France.

But Hearst's greatest quarry was Bradenstoke Priory, in Wiltshire. In 1929 the medieval tithe barn was taken down stone by stone amid great secrecy; the workmen did not even know who was employing them. The western range of the cloister, including the prior's lodging and the refectory, soon followed. All that was left above ground were two fourteenth-century undercrofts (crypts) and a tower. The magnificent early fourteenth-century double collar-beam roof of the refectory was fitted into a specially devised hall, which functioned as an 'assembly room', on the south side of the castle. Part of the outer curtain wall was demolished to accommodate it, and the windows from the prior's lodging were built into the walls. Questions were asked in Parliament as to whether an American millionaire could be allowed to jumble the national heritage in this way …

SPAB – the Society for the Protection of Ancient Buildings – was outraged. It went to the unprecedented lengths of putting up posters in London Underground stations showing before and after photographs. 'Protect your ancient buildings' ran the slogan. 'Bradenstoke, Wilts, before and during demolition for the sake of old materials.' It was found to be actionable, so the words 'for the sake of old materials' had to be pasted over with pieces of white paper. Letters of protest were published in *The Times*. 'It is more than an ordinary act of vandalism; it is an attack on the soul-life of our people,' wrote the classicist and Oxford academic Lewis Farnell. A. R. Powys, secretary of SPAB, adopted a patient, schoolmasterly tone in appealing to Hearst's better feelings. 'England at present suffers much from the removal of old buildings and fittings from places where they were originally set,' he explained; 'but it must be said that this damage to our heritage is more the result of our own people than that of the citizens of the United States of America. My society asks Mr Hearst to set Englishmen a good example in this instance, to shame them, perhaps, into better behaviour.'

Hearst was inured to worse things than this; Theodore Roosevelt had called him 'an unspeakable blackguard' who combined 'all the worst faults of the conscienceless, corrupt and dissolute monied man', and some people used stronger epithets. Miss Head was handling the SPAB correspondence. 'Mr Hearst and I are well aware of your views,' she wrote primly, '… you must please allow us to hold our own opinions.' Allom tried to pour oil on troubled waters by stating publicly that, since it would cost too much to restore the Bradenstoke barn where it was, it would be erected as part of St Donat's, replacing a modern wing 'which is incongruous and hurtful to the artistic sense'. At least it would not be lost forever, he said; but it was. The barn was not incorporated. Only the doors and windows of the prior's lodgings and the roof of the guest house were used. The barn simply disappeared, and to this day nobody knows what became of it.

There were two other barns at St Donat's. They were used as smaller versions of the Bronx warehouses and stored bits of old buildings for which no immediate use could be found. They still held a number of pieces in 1945, including thirty-three cases containing a tracery window from St Albans cathedral, 'returned from Los Angeles'.

In its heyday, a staff of forty was employed at the castle, although that did not deter Hearst from bringing chefs from London's Savoy and Claridge's while he was there. The heyday, however, did not survive the Depression. In 1937, it was decided that the castle would have to be sold – somewhat easier said that done, even at a price of £100,000, about a third of the sum that had been spent on it over the previous dozen years. There were no buyers. The last celebrity guest to stay there in the Hearst era was the American comedian Bob Hope, during a golf championship at Porthcawl in 1951. Hearst died the same year.

OPPOSITE TOP LEFT: William Randolph Hearst (second from left), with three of his sons (left to right) William, George and Randolph, in fancy dress at his birthday party in Santa Monica, California. 1938.

OPPOSITE TOP RIGHT Hearst with Julia Morgan, architect of San Simeon. Perhaps fortunately, she was too far away to advise on St Donat's.

OPPOSITE BOTTOM Hearst hosts a dinner party at San Simeon, amid trappings of historical splendour but (San Simeon being a ranch) with ketchup bottles on the table.

ABOVE Hearst, Churchill and Louis B Mayer on the MGM lot, 1929. 'I got to like him,' Churchill wrote to his wife Clementine of Hearst, 'a grave simple child – no doubt a nasty temper – playing with the most costly toys. A vast income always overspent: ceaseless building and collecting … oriental hospitalities, extreme personal courtesy (to us at any rate) and the appearance of a Quaker elder – or perhaps better Mormon elder.'

LADY BAILLIE

AT

LEEDS CASTLE

ven William Randolph Hearst thought Leeds Castle would be too much for him. Located in Kent, the Garden of England, halfway between London and the Channel port of Dover, it might have struck anyone with a British rather than an American sense of distance as considerably more convenient than South Wales, as well as incomparably romantic. Even today, the castle arises from its parkland like an Arthurian vision, seeming to hover above the broad lake or mere, formed out of the river Len. The great connoisseur of castles Martin Conway called it 'the loveliest castle in the world'.

PREVIOUS PAGES
Leeds Castle, Kent: a royal possession from the time of Edward I until the Tudor period, it was often given to the queen of the day.

Lady Baillie: probably a tough opponent at croquet.

The woman who took it on, the Hon. Olive Lady Baillie, was described, in her obituary in *The Times*, as a person of the 'sweetest and warmest womanly feelings', which may have come as a surprise to some who knew her; they would, however, have recognised that she possessed an 'immensely strong character'.[1] The latter was certainly needed to turn Leeds Castle, breathtakingly beautiful but in a hopelessly unmodernised and dilapidated state, into a functioning home, to which carefully selected parties of thirty romping guests, who included politicians, actors, artists, film and stage stars, mixed with an assortment of old friends, might descend at weekends. Lady Baillie was both elegant and steely: Leeds Castle suited her down to the glassy surface of the moat.

Leeds had been built in 1278 by another sweet and womanly lady, Queen Eleanor of Castile. She was the wife of Edward I, so mourned at her death in Lincolnshire in 1290 that the King returned from his mission against the Scots to escort her body back to London, employing his best masons to build an elaborate cross at each place that the cortège stopped overnight. The Gloriette belongs to her period, the unusual name implying a particularly sumptuous set of apartments. It occupies one of two islands in the middle of a mere, or lake, whose reflections are an essential part of the magic that Leeds works on lovers of the picturesque. The bailey stands on the other island, connected to the Gloriette by a barbican bridge, the whole complex being surrounded by a curtain wall with D-shaped towers. After Eleanor, Leeds became a property of five further queens.

OPPOSITE Sir Adrian Baillie with his mother, the dowager Lady Baillie (left), and his wife, Lady Baillie (centre). Lady Baillie was born Olive Paget; her father, Almeric Paget, was a grandson of the Marquess of Anglesey who commanded the British cavalry at the Battle of Waterloo. He worked as a cowboy in Iowa before marrying the heiress Pauline Whitney.

ABOVE Leeds Castle occupies two islands. On the left is the late thirteenth-century Gloriette (a Spanish term used of the keep); Fiennes Wykeham-Martin commissioned the architect William Baskett to build the New Castle, on the right, in the 1822–3.

Henry VIII modernised the castle and stopped there, with a retinue of 5,000, on his way to the Field of Cloth of Gold in France. The romantically named Maiden's Tower was built at some point in the same century, to be romanticised later. A Jacobean owner demolished the bailey and turned Leeds into a country house, but, even so, the next two centuries saw a decline. French and Dutch prisoners of war, housed in the Gloriette in the 1660s, set fire to it, causing a gash to develop in the walls. The fashionable Gothick makeover given to the Jacobean house in the mid-eighteenth century only went skin deep. 'A more ruinous disfigurement was perhaps never perpetrated,' fumed Charles Wykeham Martin.[2] He had reason to be angry. His father, having inherited the estate in 1821, had sunk much of the family fortune into restoring it. The Jacobean mansion was replaced with the New Castle, in an appropriately stone and castellated style, and the shape of Leeds Castle was set. Charles, having married well, was able to restore the Martin finances. An appealing description has been left by Alice Pollock, niece of the Victorian owner Philip Wykeham-Martin, who arrived by railway, a train kept waiting for them when they changed at Reading, the guard running across the station with a whistle in his mouth to usher them into a carriage.

There were various stuffed animals including a large pike, 32 lbs, with a carp in its mouth. It had been found drowned, choked by the carp.[3]

If the lake was frozen they would skate on it. At other times, they were instructed in fishing by the head gamekeeper, who bit off parts of the worms that he kept in his mouth as bait. A 19-lb pike was caught out of one of the windows. Indoors, they played ghosts, nearly frightening 'a housemaid out of her wits', and giving their nursery maid 'the fright

OPPOSITE Etienne Drian's group
portrait shows Lady Baillie with
the two daughters from her first
marriage, it was painted soon after
the Second World War. Lady Baillie
continued to decorate Leeds Castle
into the 1960s, during years when
other country houses were in crisis.

of her life'.[4] Delightful children. But after a century in the family's hands, Leeds had to
be sold to pay death duties. In 1926, it caught the imagination of Lady Baillie and her then
husband, Arthur Wilson Filmer.

Lady Baillie had been born Olive Paget in 1899. Her father, Almeric Paget, was a
grandson of the Marquess of Anglesey, who had commanded the British cavalry at the
Battle of Waterloo in 1815. But as the sixth son of a general, he left Harrow practically
penniless. Having worked in the fitting shop of the Midland Railway Company, he tried
his luck as a cowboy in Iowa. Although unusually well connected for the prairie, and
sometimes absent for house parties or games of cricket, he could still knuckle down, at
one point buying a soap factory which used the by-products of slaughtered pigs.[5] He made
a fortune as an industrialist, became a successful yachtsman, an MP and treasurer of the
League of Nations; during the First World War he founded the Military Massage Service,
providing a forerunner of physiotherapy for troops. In 1918 he was raised to the peerage
as Baron Queenborough. One of Paget's enterprises had been to establish the Dominion
Coal Company with Henry Melville Whitney. In 1895, he married Whitney's niece, the
heiress Pauline Whitney; President Grover Cleveland attended the wedding.

Olive was born in New York in 1899 and educated in France. Although she claimed
to think of herself as British, and married three British husbands, all of whom she
divorced, contemporaries assumed that, like her money, she was American. Glorying in
Leeds Castle purely for the sake of its aesthetic appeal and historic resonance, as Lords
Curzon or Conway might have done, was not enough. It also had to form the setting of a
comfortable, smart and private existence, which was notably different from the life of
most British chatelaines during the bleak 1930s, let alone the decades of near despair that
followed the Second World War.

Her first marriage was to the Hon. Charles Winn, second son of Lord St Oswald, in
1919. It ended in 1925, and she married Wilson Filmer later the same year. She bought
Leeds Castle in 1926. Five years later, the Wilson Filmer marriage also having collapsed,
she became Lady Baillie, having wed Sir Adrian Baillie, 6th Baronet – 'tall, very good-
looking, with a natural baritone voice, [and] a real understanding of music', as Diana
Tauber, wife of the tenor Richard, remembered him. Although the Baillies divorced in
1944, Olive retained the name. None of her husbands, though, emerges as more than a
cipher beside their adamantine wife. Sir Adrian was treated as a child. In Monte Carlo,
Lady Baillie was a big player, while her husband, whom she did not want to gamble, was
despatched to nightclubs with pretty girls. There
was also gambling at Leeds.

In her shimmering white dress, as sleek and
apparently boneless as an eel, Lady Baillie – at
least as she appears in the portrait with the two
daughters from her first marriage, painted by
Etienne Drian after the Second World War –
personified the smart look of the 1930s. It was
augmented by the mahogany cigarette holder which

Although she claimed to think of herself as British,
and married three British husbands, all of whom she
divorced, contemporaries assumed that, like her
money, she was American.

was forever between her fingers. To the press she was completely unapproachable. Even
her guests found her so reserved that they might not so much as meet her for a couple
of days. Her mornings were spent in her room. Lunch was an informal affair. At other
times, she liked to be closeted with the powerful, from the German ambassador to the
Court of St James's, Joachim von Ribbentrop, to senior British politicians. When David
Niven spent a weekend at Leeds Castle at the beginning of the Second World War, he
found 'some of the big wheels of government at play', including David Margesson, the
Tory Chief Whip – Geoffrey Lloyd, Minister of Transport – and 'Crinks' Johnston, leader
of the Liberal Party. He found them uncongenial.[6] Both Margesson and Lloyd were
reputed to be Olive's lovers.[7] The moral tone at Leeds was louche, with 'lots of corridor-
creeping'.[8] Niven was part of the leavening mix of guests which included Errol Flynn,
James Stewart and other movie stars.

How much power Lady Baillie wielded cannot be quantified. It was probably small,
but she liked the aroma of it. Meanwhile, her house parties had everything to amuse
guests. Activities included golf, tennis, squash, croquet, boating or skating on the moat
according to season, and horses; with picnics in the park in fine weather, and a cinema in

RIGHT In the dining room, the tapestries of birds and flowers reflected Lady Baillie's love of birds, for which she made a duckery and aviaries in the grounds. Her collection of Australian parakeets was famous.

BELOW Lady Baillie's bedroom at Leeds is an immaculate example of Stephane Boudin's style. The paneling was distressed with wire brushes before painting to make it look old.

the Maiden's Tower for those who had had enough fresh air. Dinner would be served at eight. It said something about Lady Baillie's attitude to her guests that it might be delayed for an hour while she failed to appear, more interesting matters having gained her attention. Afterwards there would be cards, or the carpet rolled back for dancing to music from a gramophone.

The castle became as chic as its chatelaine. With her American money and love of France – she spoke French flawlessly – it was perhaps natural that her taste should not have been confined to the conventions of English decorating. There were as yet no listed building controls to stop an owner doing what he or she liked to a castle, however ancient. Work started on the Gloriette, which, under the hand of monsieur Rateau, was kitted out in expensive French Gothic flavour, including a seemingly antique and appropriately distressed spiral staircase made in Paris and reconstructed on site. Cupboards and wardrobes had built-in lighting.

After her American friend Audrey Emery, who was married to the Grand Duke Dmitri Pavlovich of Russia, introduced her to Stéphane Boudin in 1933, she transferred her patronage to him. Boudin worked for Maison Jansen, established in 1880. We have met him before at Ditchley, and he shall reappear, *con brio* and *con amore*, at 'Chips' Channon's 5 Belgrave Square. Other clients included the Duke and Duchess of Windsor, the Charles Wrightsmans, Stavros Niarchos, the Gianni Agnellis and Jacqueline Kennedy, under whose auspices Boudin restored portions of the White House. But Leeds would remain unrivalled for its longevity as a commission, Boudin working there for thirty years.

One of Jansen's strengths was its atelier. There, expert craftsmen could make, improve or adapt anything that was needed in a palatial abode. This included both old boiseries, which could be extended and fitted to new rooms as required, and elaborate *passementerie*: the fabulously intricate and expensive textile trimmings which could be seen in the richest of French interiors, but were generally thought to be too expensive or too showy for the English country house. Examples of both were installed into Leeds, the Yellow Drawing Room, which replaced a room that Rateau had fitted with grey oak, being given what is known as a *lambrequin*, an ornamental drapery around the top of the room (French words have to be used to describe ultra-luxurious textiles because they have no English equivalent). The elegant panelling of the dining room, painted in duck-egg blue, framed exceptionally pretty tapestries of birds and flowers, which brought to mind the

TOP The library which Boudin designed in 1938. Like other British country-house libraries, it was intended to be comfortable as well as bookish; the touches of red morocco glaze on the cream-coloured bookcases reflect the colour of bindings – an attention to aesthetic detail that was uncommon on the British side of the Channel.

ABOVE One of a pair of painted commodes purchased from Jansen by Lady Baillie for the Cream Bedroom in 1937. The trompe-l'oeil decoration depicts music.

RIGHT Leeds Castle remains one of the most romantic buildings in Britain.

exotic birds that Lady Baillie introduced to the park. Under the transforming magic of Boudin's craftsmen, scraping paint with wire brushes, hanging ostrich-plume wallpaper and reconditioning ancient needlework, the castle glowed with colour like a jewel box.[9]

Contemporaries must have been astonished to see such costly work continuing into the 1960s, with little regard for the collapse of aristocratic life on both sides of the Channel after the Second World War. Many of them would have agreed with H. V. Morton when he looked around, paying half a crown to charity, as part of a tour that became his book *I Saw Two Englands*. As he lay on a grass bank and admired the Gloriette, he was moved by the 'enormous' scale and brilliant white stone. But the last thing in the world he would have wanted to do was to own it.

> I thought how remarkable it is in these days, when incomes can pay more than ten shillings in the pound income tax and people are less inclined than ever to assume responsibility, that anyone can be found who loves this old castle sufficiently to keep life within its walls.

Lady Baillie did. The castle is now preserved, with the major rooms as she left them, as a Foundation.

ABOVE The banqueting hall, created for the visit of Henry VIII and Catherine of Aragon on May 22, 1520, while going to Dover, was enhanced with a Caen stone fireplace by Lady Baillie's first French decorator, Armand-Albert Rateau.

OPPOSITE Staircase by Armand-Albert Rateau, with pleasingly time-worn treads. Rateau was Lady Baillie's second designer at Leeds, following architect Owen Little who was responsible for some ancillary buildings and structural work. This staircase was swept away by Rateau's replacement Stéphane Boudin.

THE
PRINCE OF WALES
& WALLIS SIMPSON

AT

FORT BELVEDERE

'What could you possibly want that queer old place for?' growled King George V when his son Edward, Prince of Wales, asked him for a grace and favour house on the edge of Windsor Great Park in 1930. 'Those damn weekends, I suppose.'[1] It was a revealing comment. Weekends, a shocking novelty to Victorian hostesses, had become a social commonplace at the beginning of the twentieth century, when fewer men could afford to spend a week or more in the country at a time, and the 'here today, in next week tomorrow' of the motorcar enabled guests to travel further than they could have done by horse. The King, though, was stuck in the Edwardian age – that of his father. The Prince of Wales would become Edward VIII, promising another but quite different Edwardian age. The tone would be progressive, unstuffy and, in part, American; it was an American who gave him the confidence of his convictions which, with a Prince of Wales-ly aptitude to vacillate, he had previously lacked. His obsession with his American wife put an end to his short reign as Edward VIII. The denouement took place at that the 'queer old place' that so much expressed his personality, to the extent that, like himself, it had come under Wallis Simpson's rule: Fort Belvedere.

PREVIOUS PAGE The Duke and Duchess of Windsor make the best of it on September 3,1939 after their return from France at the start of World War II. They were photographed at their temporary home near Ashdown Forest, Sussex.

Fort Belvedere, originally one of the caprices of Virginia Water, built for the Duke of Cumberland in the 1750s.

Edward had a natural affinity with the United States. His first North American tour had taken place in 1919. Canada put out the flags. 'I've never received such a welcome!' he wrote from Toronto to his mistress Freda Dudley Ward, herself half American through her mother. 'It's been too marvellous for words … knocks Cardiff or any place in Great Britain right out.'[2] He had met Americans, generally liked them and was 'just longing to go to the States'. Characteristically, the King was against the US leg of the tour, but did not veto it. He went to Washington and New York, dancing with senators' daughters and attending war workers' dinners, and generally catching what diplomats called the American spirit. The US played to the Prince's strengths. Easy to get along with, he excelled when making personal contact with people, whoever they might be. The States suited his spontaneous style; he could for once escape the protocol that he found so irksome. Furthermore, the American press liked the sight of a young man enjoying himself. If he overdid it, that was part of his democratic appeal. He was, in 1919, still boyish, but it was a different matter when New York was given longer exposure to him in 1924, on the second visit. Overdoing it was taken too far this time, with drink, women and the wrong set all too much in evidence. Edward was now thirty; what had previously been accepted as the follies of youth did not look so well in a man approaching early middle age. But the magic of his personality, combined with the glamour of his position, overcame the indiscretions, and he was, in the newspeak of the day, 'Swamped by Adoring Throngs'.

A pretty St Louis debutante named Lenore Cahill summed up the impression made by the Prince after dancing all night with him on the liner going over: 'He seemed exactly like an attractive young American.'[3] The informality of American life was refreshing, after the fossilised rigidity of his father's court. His wardrobe came to include sporting clothes in plangent checks, pullovers of vibrant hues: such garments were not the recommended wear of Savile Row. He favoured soft collars, and began to affect an American accent in preference to the previously fashionable faux cockney. He liked cocktails rather too much. In London, he consorted with Emerald Cunard and had known 'Chips' Channon since 1920; and he attended Lady Baillie's bed-hopping weekends at Leeds Castle. A 'rather-tough looking American' man who quizzed Osbert Sitwell about the Prince, turned out to see him regularly, perhaps chez Lady Cunard's rival, Laura Corrigan.[4] And in the late 1920s, Thelma Furness, who, having ditched the first husband whom she had unwisely married at sixteen, was now the neglected wife of swaggering, foul-mouthed Lord Furness, became more than a friend. Lady Furness replaced Mrs Dudley Ward as the Prince's inamorata. When, in 1928, they went on safari in Kenya

together, with Lord Furness in tow, they always found their tents next to each other at the end of the line. As Lady Furness recalled in her memoirs, they shared a campfire — and more besides. She was hedonistic, constantly reinvented herself, and, unlike the Prince's British women friends, felt no constitutional imperative to contain the natural waywardness of the heir to the throne. Fort Belvedere would be a statement of the Prince's own desire to establish a different persona, in a free and easy setting that had more in common with the life of the American rich than with the 'Buckhouse prison', as he referred to Buckingham Palace.

Until 1930, the Prince's only residence had been York House in London, which he felt to be 'more an office than a home'. While convenient for the 'metropolitan amenities', such as the Embassy Club, he claimed to be 'a man who loved the country'. Since the mid-1920s he had rented various country houses, where he liked to play golf; he now wanted a place of his own. Being out of the public eye — and the lenses of the increasingly intrusive press — must have been part of it. A sentimentalist at heart, the Prince liked being near the scenes of his childhood, having 'paddled in rowboats with Mary and my brothers' on Virginia Water, which lay at the end of a gentle slope. Although tucked away, in a dense growth of laurels and yew trees, it was so close to London that he could make out the dome of St Paul's Cathedral through a telescope. It was also a good place from which to appreciate Windsor Castle, which he had found forbidding and oppressive when growing up; distance lent enchantment to the view.

Fort Belvedere enters documented history in 1757. It was then a triangular tower, with a hexagonal turret at each corner: one of the caprices of Virginia Water made for the Duke of Cumberland, the Ranger of Windsor

ABOVE The Duke and Duchess of Windsor, with their dogs, a pug and a terrier, outside the Seminole Club in Palm Beach, Florida.

OPPOSITE Prince as Polo Player. This photograph of the future Edward VIII suggests both his glamour and his weakness of character. Part of Wallis Simpson's irresistible appeal for him was the strength of her personality and her willingness to talk straight.

The States suited his spontaneous style; he could for once escape the protocol that he found so irksome. Furthermore, the American press liked the sight of a young man enjoying himself. If he overdid it, that was part of his democratic appeal.

LEFT The hexagonal domed hall which was part of the original Belvedere, built in the 1750s; the domed ceiling dates from 1929–30. The colours in the photograph were pale grey-pink, lemon and white.

BELOW The dining room, with mural fantasies of Windsor and Harewood. The decoration exorcised memories of the Duke of Windsor, in whose time the walls were panelled and hung with historic pictures.

OPPOSITE The windows of the so-called Queen's Bedroom in the bow that was added to Fort Belvedere by Sir Jeffry Wyattville for George IV in the late 1820s. At the time this photograph was taken in 1959, Fort Belvedere was occupied by the Hon. Gerald Lascelles, a grandson of George V.

ABOVE Fort Belvedere was planned along American lines as a pleasure and sports complex. Amenities included swimming pool (bottom right), tennis court (bottom left) and stable (top left). The King had a private airfield three miles away, near, as the American magazine *Life* noted in 1936, Queen Victoria's grave.

OPPOSITE Fort Belvedere, denuded of the jungly rhododendrons which the Prince of Wales delighted in slashing down. A fort only by name, the building here looks all too vulnerable to outside forces.

Great Park, which included the launching of a Chinese junk, or 'Mandarin Yacht', George IV had employed Sir Jeffry Wyattville to transform it into a toy fort in 1827-28, completing the illusion by housing the Duke of Cumberland's collection of guns there. An increasingly ancient bombardier was employed to fire them – rather as a royal equivalent of Wemmick's canon in David Copperfield – until the post was abolished in 1910. Wyattville linked the Flag Tower to one called the Magazine Tower. A projecting one-storey dining room was built, octagonal in shape. (This became the Prince of Wales' drawing room.) Quarters for a caretaker and the bombardier were also provided. In the years before 1929, Fort Belvedere had been occupied by Lieutenant Colonel Sir Malcolm Murray of the Seaforth Highlanders, Deputy Ranger of Windsor Great Park, who was to die in a boating accident on Virginia Water in 1938. While adequate for Murray, it was not good enough for the Prince of Wales, who proceeded to make it his 'independent home' – a status for which, when he became King, there had been no exact precedent, according to the Christopher Hussey.[5]

'Fixing up' The Fort, as he called Fort Belvedere, became a joy and a passion. It reflected his own ideas:

> And, being mine, they were modern. Inside I introduced, to the extent that space and the old walls allowed, many of the creature conveniences that I had sampled and enjoyed in the New World – a bathroom to nearly every room, showers, a steam bath, built-in cupboards, central heating – the so-called modern comforts that were seldom found in profusion in British houses.

According to Hussey, the Prince was aided in tackling the interior by Mrs Dudley Ward, presumably not quite yet seen off by Lady Furness. By 1959, the only room still to bear the imprint of these years was the drawing room, its walls surfaced and painted to represent pinewood panelling, in the manner of a Scottish shooting lodge. The cost of the repairs, plumbing and redecoration was £21,000.

The Prince had his domestic side. Since childhood, he had practised needlework, which he called his 'secret vice'. But the aspect of The Fort's revival which most appealed to him was the garden. Swathes of it had to be cleared. He learnt how to use a billhook and set about the laurels, taking out his frustration with the world as he slashed them down. It became a completely absorbing activity. For a time he preferred it to fox-hunting and even golf. Sometimes he would not even stop for lunch: a footman would bring out a cup of tea and an apple, sounding his presence with a whistle; the Prince would whistle back, and so they would continue until they found each other. Gardening engrossed Edward's weekends:

I was in such a hurry to make the place over that I begrudged as lost a daylight hour that did not see the work progressing. Saturday afternoons and Sundays, when my gardeners were off, I pressed my weekend guests into arduous physical labour to which some of them were unaccustomed. Groaning and grunting, they joined me in hacking out the underbrush, pruning trees, and transplanting shrubs; but presently they began to share my enthusiasm. Even my brother Bertie, who lived nearby in the Great Park at Royal Lodge, would drop over to lend a hand.

An outside swimming pool was constructed in 1931-32; a hard tennis court made alongside the battery. The Fort came to resemble the sports complexes with which rich men's country places in the United States were equipped.

Sometimes he played the bagpipes, sometimes the ukulele. He could smoke, relax and, if he wanted, throw gramophone records about the place, to see if they really lived up to their manufacturer's claim of being unbreakable. For someone who was otherwise almost always in the public eye, or under that of his family, it was a release. Here he could entertain whom he chose, how he chose. Among the guests was Wallis Simpson.

History cannot decide what Lady Furness meant when, needing to return to the United States for her sister Gloria Vanderbilt's trial in 1934, she asked Mrs Simpson to take care of the Prince. Was she being naive or was she simply tired of him? Or had she failed to recognise the challenge posed by the angular woman with the big hands who, until that moment, had apparently been her closest friend in London? Mrs Simpson knew what she wanted and did not take prisoners. Life in London with the dull and not particularly prosperous Ernest Simpson, her second husband, had not been a social triumph. They lived in a rented flat and had to worry about bills. Like everyone else, they were conscious that a connection with the Prince, whom they had first met in January 1931, would elevate their standing. By mid-1934, Wallis had Edward to herself. By early the next year, two rooms at The Fort were being turned into one for her benefit: 'presumably to obviate the risk that, when the house was full, the dressing room adjoining her bedroom might be occupied and access thus impeded'.[6] It was not, according to Philip Ziegler, her personality, appearance or sexual technique that captivated the Prince, but her complete indifferent to the royal aura that doth hedge a king:

Wallis respected neither office nor man, and made it abundantly plain that this was so. No Englishwoman, however assertive, however independent, however little wedded to the cause of monarchy, could have done the same.

Her withering comments after the guests had left Fort Belvedere could reduce him to tears. Mrs Simpson spent almost every weekend at The Fort, presiding over a guest list that consisted of 'courtiers and diplomats, American men of affairs and English Society, garnished with a sprinkling of statesmen, soldiers and sailors'.[7] After the Prince became King, more alterations were carried out under the aegis of Giles Gilbert Scott, prominent if only as the architect of Battersea Power Station, south London, and the iconic red telephone box. When Mrs Simpson received poison pen letters during the Abdication Crisis, she moved to Fort Belvedere permanently. Permanently, that is, until 3 December 1936, when, after a melancholy supper, she walked through the King's bedroom and out on to the lawn, without saying goodbye to any of the staff, but taking her jewellery. The abdication papers were signed by Edward VIII and his three brothers at Fort Belvedere a week later. 'Like a swimmer surfacing from a great depth,' the Duke of Windsor would recall, 'I left the room and stepped outside, inhaling the fresh morning air.'[8]

The Duke of Windsor, as he now was, may have hoped to return once the dust had settled, but his brother, now King George VI, was by no means anxious to have him living on British soil. The Fort languished for nearly twenty years until a ninety-nine-year lease was sold in 1955 to the Hon. Gerald Lascelles and his actress wife Angela Dowding, Lascelles being a grandson of George V. The house ceased to be a royal home. One of the recent owners is Galen Weston, the Canadian billionaire, philanthropist and polo patron, whose many and diverse business interests include Fortnum & Mason.

'CHIPS' CHANNON

AT

5 BELGRAVE SQUARE &

KELVEDON HALL

'I have flair, intuition, great good taste but only second-rate ambition,' confided Henry 'Chips' Channon to his diary on 19 July 1935. 'I am far too susceptible to flattery; I hate and am uninterested in all the things most men like such as sport, business, statistics, debates, speeches, war and the weather; but I am riveted by lust, furniture, glamour and society and jewels.' Chips became an MP but did not rise beyond being parliamentary private secretary to the Foreign Office under secretary, R. A. Butler, but some of the very qualities which Chips identified as an obstacle to success in public life made him shine in the arrangement of houses. The decoration of a single room at 5 Belgrave Square, the home that he made with his rich wife Lady Honor Guinness, cost as much as a country house. That sparkling interrerior, as is so often the way with decorative schemes, has been swept away, but photographs, which do scant justice by themselves, are brought to life by the diaries for which Chips is famous. Surviving for the years 1918, 1923–28 and 1934–53, they are as vivid, in their own way, as those of Samuel Pepys: soufflé more than plum pudding.

PREVIOUS PAGES Chips with dog at 5 Belgrave Square. Above the fireplace hangs a portrait of him with his beloved son Paul, who became a cabinet minister in the Thatcher government.

Chips had been born in 1897 (although he liked to pretend it was 1899) in Chicago. His father owned a fleet of boats plying the Great Lakes. The First World War took him to Paris, where he arrived in 1917, with the American Red Cross. Whatever exposure he may have had in the French capital to the aristocratic milieu depicted by Marcel Proust was reinforced by a year and a half at Oxford University. It was there that he acquired the sobriquet Chips, which he so thoroughly adopted, in preference to Henry, that it became his telegraphic address (although in 1957, towards the end of his life, he was knighted as Sir Henry). He became a popinjay and flagrant social climber, characteristics that did not endear him to everyone: the politician and diplomat Duff Cooper regarded him as 'a toady'; those who were susceptible to his charm, wit and talent for throwing a good party, however, took them in good part, as being inseparable from one of London's most amusing spirits. Cooper's wife, Lady Diana, a daughter of the Duke of Rutland, took a more generous view of him than her husband: 'Never was there a surer or more enlivening friend,' she wrote.

ABOVE LEFT Lady Honor Guinness marries Chips Channon on 14th July 1933.

OPPOSITE Belgrave Square, the grandest of the squares in Belgravia, laid out by Thomas Cubitt on the Duke of Westminster's estate in the 1820s. Chips and Lady Honor acquired 5 Belgrave Square in 1935 and had it expensively decorated by Stephane Boudin.

He installed the mighty in his gilded chairs and exalted the humble. He made the old and tired, the young and strong, shine beneath his thousand lighted candles. Without stint he gave of his riches and of his compassion.

Chips found Europe, especially the Europe of aristocratic and aesthetic excess, altogether more congenial than the puritanical United States, which he regarded as crass. His passionate desire to preserve it led him to support appeasement during the rise of Nazi Germany, initially because he hoped that Hitler might have intended to restore the monarchy, the House of Hohenzollern. Chips was devoted to his son Paul, but his marriage failed after Lady Honor left him for a Czech airman, and he found a soulmate in Peter Coates, who would become the gardening editor of *House and Garden* in 1948, a position that he kept for over half a century.

On 23 March 1935, Chips and Lady Honor made the decision to buy 5 Belgrave Square:

It is not too grand and is dirt cheap compared with all the other houses we have seen. It has a distinguished air and we will make it gay and comfortable. We hope to be living there by 1 September. I think it is just possible. It will be fun arranging it …

Since Thomas Cubitt's Belgrave Square, on the Duke of Westminster's Belgravia estate, a short walk from Buckingham Palace, has been regarded as one of the best London addresses since it was laid out in the 1820s, that 'not too grand' was only comparative. Designed by the neoclassicist George Basevi, killed in 1845 by a fall from the tower of Ely Cathedral while he was surveying it, the exterior of the house is chastely classical. Chaste was not the note that Chips wanted to sound inside, however. Like Nancy Lancaster and Lady Baillie, he employed Stéphane Boudin to create a dining room inspired by the riotous rococo of the Amalienburg pavilion in the Nymphenburg Palace, Munich, designed by François de Cuvilliés 200 years earlier. As he gushed on 17 June, 'It will be a symphony in blue and silver … cascades of aquamarine. Will it be London's loveliest room or is my flame dead?' Chips knew Munich well, having published a biography of Wagner's patron entitled *The Ludwigs of Bavaria* two years before. The frothy exuberance of south German rococo provided an objective correlative to his personality.

On 6 July, the Channons spent the whole day with Monsieur Boudin. 'He is

TOP LEFT AND PREVIOUS
PAGE RIGHT The dining room at
5 Belgrave Square, designed by
Stephane Boudin. Chips described
it as a 'symphony in blue and silver...
cascades of aquamarine. Will it be
London's loveliest room or is my
flame dead?'.

ABOVE Torchbearers – one Nubian,
the other Chinese – flanked the
approach to the new dining room.

LEFT Lady Honor Channon's
bedroom. The modernist aesthetic
of the 1930s is reflected in
the austerity of a room, which
nevertheless contains a fine Empire
bed. The bedside table, in matching
taste, supports a telephone.

considered the greatest decorator in the world,' Chips recorded. 'There is to be a small ante-room opening into a gallery – orange and silver like the Amalienburg; then another door, and then I hope, stupefaction – a high banqueting hall, all blue and silver.'

On 28 July, he again revelled in the effect that it would have on his guests, in the Depression-struck 1930s: 'It will shock, and perhaps stagger London. And will cost us over £6,000.' Inevitably, the initial time frame had been optimistic, and it was not until 1 February 1936 that he could sleep 'for the first time in my new, white, modern Biedermeyer room'. The house smelt strongly of paint.

The ideal guest was Harold Nicolson, to judge from his response on first seeing the redecorated house, which was exactly what Chips would have wished for:

> Oh my God how rich and powerful Lord Channon has become! There is his house in Belgrave Square next door to Prince George, Duke of Kent, and Duchess of ditto and little Prince Edward. The house is all Regency upstairs with very carefully draped curtains and Madame Récamier sofas and wall paintings. Then the dining-room is entered through an orange lobby and discloses itself suddenly as a copy of the blue room of the Amelienburg near Munich – baroque and rococo and what-ho and oh-no-no and all that. Very fine indeed.

Writing in *Country Life*, Christopher Hussey chose more measured words to describe a similar response. Since 1918, many of the great palaces of London had been demolished, along with swathes of Georgian terraces; only the year after the Channons had moved into 5 Belgrave Square, the Georgian Group was founded to oppose the despoliation. Here, though, was a London house in the rudest state of good health. Refreshingly, for those who loved architecture, the Channons had taken a stand against the prevailing spirit of the age.

On 28 April 1937, Chips records lunching with 'Colebox' – the society hostess Lady Colefax – with 'a pleasant party', including the bisexual Lord David Cecil and the homosexual architect Gerald Wellesley, who later became 7th Duke of Wellington:

In addition to drownings in the lake, falls from windows and the death of pupils from minor accidents, the house had grown grim with neglect.

'They talked of a country house, Kelvedon Hall, near Kelvedon Hatch. I am intrigued about it and shall look at it. Will it prove only one more dream to toy with for a few weeks and then discard, from inertia?'

Like 5 Belgrave Square, Kelvedon was a solid, uninspiring house, which only the eye of a dedicated improver would have viewed with partiality. For the previous five years it had housed a Catholic school, 'during which period', observed *Country Life*, 'a series of unlucky mischances had given the red Georgian house a slightly sinister reputation in the eyes of the neighbours'. In addition to drownings in the lake, falls from windows and the death of pupils from minor accidents, the house had grown grim with neglect. But the Channons saw potential. In an entry the next month, characteristically headed 'Coronation Eve' (George VI had ascended the throne after Edward VIII's abdication), Chips recorded that their offer of £5,000 for Kelvedon had been accepted. He now had a new role to act up to, that of 'a Squire of Essex'.

According to his diaries, Chips loved the bucolic idyll. 'Glorious weather and we lunched out of doors,' he wrote on 10 April 1939, 'basked in the sun and Honor and I actually plunged into the water. Afterwards Paul and I caught frogs together. Kelvedon is a dream of fruit blossom and spring loveliness – war seems really unthinkable.' War, however, would become all too real; and the Channons' marriage would soon be over. Although, typically, Chips continued to view rural life as through the prism of Humperdinck's operetta *Hansel and Gretel*, the responsibilities of looking after the house, even for a man as gilded as Chips, began to outweigh the pleasures. The Channons were still together on a 'lovely' early September weekend but the mood was not bright:

> There were endless decisions to be made; papers to be stored; fuss and confusion; irritated servants; neglected dogs; plate-room and cellar complications. We packed up all our jewelled toys, the Fabergé bibelots and gold watches, etc., and counted the wine, then we welcomed 160 refugees, all nice East End people, but Honor was depressed and worn out, and our Sunday not as happy as I had hoped.

There was a meet of hunt and hounds at the house that December, and the place lifted Chips's spirits the next spring. But he had to bury his diaries, along with his choicest bibelots, in a tin box in the churchyard, in case of invasion, and the roar of fighter planes and enemy bombers made Essex no more tranquil than London. He still enjoyed the swimming pool (baroque) that he created, along with an 'exquisite' pavilion, but ominously headed one entry 'Kelvedon, or rather Bleak House'.

Published in the spring of 1941, the *Country Life* articles have the air of a requiem. New lodge gates, bathing pavilion and painted decoration by John Churchill cannot detract from the mournful subheading: 'The Country Home of Mr. Henry Channon, M.P.' Lady Honor had gone. The heart seemed to have gone out of the enterprise. 'A room in the south wing was also turned into an "Austrian room", with baroque furniture and brightly coloured wooden sculpture,' but the time for such frivolities had passed: not having been finished when the war began, it was now used for other purposes. With its expanses of mirror glass in the bedrooms, and Lady Honor's bedroom, made from a never-consecrated chapel, Kelvedon was not the usual country house and Chips was not the usual country squire; but neither was he quite the old Chips.

Lonely and sexually disinhibited, he came to be looked on as a grotesque after the Second World War. His knighthood was only partial compensation for failing health. Like other butterflies, his time in the sun had been brief – but colourful.

His adored Paul did not fly on such rainbow-patterned wings, but reached greater heights, serving as Trade and Industry Secretary and Transport Secretary in Margaret Thatcher's second government. How pleased Chips would have been to know that he became Baron Kelvedon when made a life peer in 1997.

ABOVE Chips (standing) entertains Terrence Rattigan, Lady Juliet Duff, the Hon. John Cooper (John Julius Norwich) and Lord Audley at 5 Belgrave Square in 1947.

J.PAUL GETTY

AT

SUTTON PLACE

The oil tycoon J. Paul Getty did not live at the Tudor mansion of Sutton Place as a recluse. He was not lonely. He found these myths 'howlingly funny', according to his autobiography. To disprove them, he published selected entries from his appointments book. Stating it in the bluntest English possible, 'if I am – as the press would have it – a recluse, then I damned well get out and around one hell of a lot more than any "recluse" in history. If I am "lonely", then I am the luckiest lonely human being on the face of the earth, for I am surrounded by dear friends and loyal business associates. If I "live alone", then the people who come to Sutton Place, often staying for weeks, must be figments of my imagination – or, more accurately, the suggestion that they are NOT there is the product of some extremely warped imaginations.'[1]

PREVIOUS PAGE The misery of riches? The American oil millionaire J. Paul Getty in the dining room of Sutton Place, circa 1960.

Getty looks no more cheerful outside his home.

He was, however, extremely mean. And rather odd. Born in 1892, Getty was not an entirely self-made man, rather 'the only son of an extremely able and successful pioneer of the American oil industry, who really did start from poverty and at his death left a fortune of $15 million, though no more than $500,000 to his son'.[2] Although he liked to play up the time he spent as a roustabout in the Oklahoma oilfields, where other workers called him Red because of the colour of his hair, that was only an occupation of the summer months. The rest of the year he spent variously at the University of Southern California, Berkeley and Oxford, the last being his favourite. There he became a friend of the Prince of Wales. He came to speak seven languages. University explains what he later called his delayed start in business at the age of twenty-two. In 1957, *Fortune* magazine identified him as the richest man in the United States, and by implication, the world.

At that time, Getty's life was spent in hotel rooms around Europe. Although he was an autocrat and the digital age had not dawned, he maintained that he did not have to be physically present in Los Angeles to run Getty Oil. In Europe, he amassed the collection of art and antiquities, particularly Renaissance paintings and classical sculpture, which would become the nucleus of the Getty Museum, opened in 1974. But as his sixties advanced, he began to see the attractions of a more settled domestic existence. The idea of a château

OPPOSITE Constructed in the early 1970s, the original part of the J. Paul Getty Museum at Pacific Palisades, California is a free replication of the Villa of the Papyri at Herculaneum. It has been suggested that Getty believed himself to be a reincarnation of the Emperor Hadrian. The Villa-Museum provided, some thought, an appropriate metaphor for the sybaritic Californian lifestyle.

THIS PAGE A bit chilly for Surrey. Perseus slays the Gorgon, at the end of a Sutton Place lawn.

Weston built a princely early Renaissance house in the favourite Tudor material of brick, then still a costly novelty, enjoyed for the flamboyance with which it could be laid; this was enriched with glazed terracotta as at Hampton Court Palace.

outside Paris was rejected after political unrest and the election of Charles de Gaulle as President made France uncongenial to a rich foreigner. A solution presented itself in 1959, when the Duke and Duchess of Sutherland invited him to dinner at his Surrey country house, 30 miles south of London: Sutton Place, near Guildford. In the course of conversation, he discovered that the Duke found it too expensive to maintain. Discreet enquiries were made, and it was revealed that the Duke was prepared to part with it for what Getty regarded as a bargain price. For him, bargains were always difficult to resist.

Sutton Place had been built by Sir Richard Weston, a courtier of Henry VIII. The estate had slipped into his hands after he had been one of the members of the jury who convicted the 3rd Duke of Buckingham, its previous owner, of treason. Weston built a princely early Renaissance house in the favourite Tudor material of brick, then still a costly novelty, enjoyed for the flamboyance with which it could be laid; this was enriched with glazed terracotta as at Hampton Court Palace. The King came; he liked to play tennis there. There may have been other games when Anne Boleyn joined him, because Weston's

ABOVE AND LEFT The gallery and the dining room at Sutton Place. Both rooms are hung with tapestries and furnished with fine oak and walnut pieces. Although Getty was presented in the media as a misanthrope, he was a highly educated collector, who surrounded himself with women, fighting for his attention.

ABOVE Staged photograph of J. Paul Getty (centre) leading the seventeen-year-old Jeanette Maxwell into dinner at a party given for her at Sutton Place in 1960. Gatecrashers (some pictured right) behaved atrociously.

son, Francis, was named as one of her lovers and beheaded, shortly before she was. Weston himself rode out the storm. The story of the romance might well have appealed to Getty who, five times divorced, always surrounded himself with women.

'A great deal of work and a considerable investment were required to renovate and refurbish Sutton Place,' noted Getty. 'The main problems were those of renovation, modernization (for example, the installation of new and up-to-date kitchen equipment and fixtures) and redecoration.'[3] Organising the work fell to the *maitresse en titre* of the moment, Mrs Penelope Kitson, known as Pen. Getty's contribution was to buy works of art. As he wrote in *The Joys of Collecting*:

The 'Great Hall', which is 57 feet long and 25 feet wide with 31-foot-high ceilings, is a perfect room in which to display Rubens' large (92½ by 72 inches) canvas of *Diana and Her Nymphs Departing for the Hunt*, which I obtained in 1961, and the 60½-inch Snyders-Boeckhorst *The Pantry*, a canvas I acquired in 1960.

The Long Gallery was equally suited to the Brussels and Flemish tapestries that were hung there. With its velvet-covered walls, the dining room lent itself to grand eighteenth-century portraits by Pompeo Battoni and Gainsborough.

There is no truth to the rumour that Getty's personal guests at Sutton Place were required to use a public telephone box when making calls. A telephone box was installed, but only for the use of builders, journalists and other people who passed through, who felt entitled to run up the richest man in the world's phone bills. Like William Randolph Hearst, Getty did not buy the country house in his own name; it was a property of Getty Oil, and the company did not consult him about the phone box. It was taken out when the works were finished. But Getty's lugubrious appearance, coupled with the ruthless cynicism with which he viewed all human motivation, pigeon-holed him in the public imagination as the millionaire who could not enjoy himself. He loved the oil business, art and women; he detested spending money – whatever the quantity – unnecessarily. He bought a second-class train ticket, rather than be chauffeur-driven from London, and kept a Scrooge-like eye on the household accounts. But he was capable of giving a house-warming party in 1960 when the restoration of Sutton Place was complete. Invitations were sent out to 1,200 people.

The party confirmed his worst view of human nature. It was awkward to refuse guests who asked if they could bring hangers-on. Worse was the problem of gatecrashers. So many people felt entitled to abuse his hospitality that, with a 3-mile queue of cars on the A3, the police gave up the attempt to check invitations. A couple of thousand people gained admittance, some of them shamelessly guzzling undue quantities of the caviar and Champagne that had been provided. Slim and courteous, the elderly host was ignored. 'It is axiomatic at a party attended by scions of the British upper class,' wrote Russell Miller in *The House of Getty*, 'that if a swimming pool is within reach, someone has to be thrown in, fully dressed.'[4] The victim on this occasion was a photographer, laden with cameras and a flash pack, who was toppled into the water by a hefty shove (his immediate fear was that he might be electrocuted by the powerful battery he was carrying). The wreckage that faced the cleaners the next morning was appalling. Tapestries had been smeared with ice cream, cigarettes left burning on fine French furniture or ground into Persian carpets, and velvet hangings ripped. As far as the public was concerned, Getty went back into his shell.

But he was far from alone. One of the conveniences of hotel life was the ease with which a succession of women could pass through Getty's existence without meeting each other. The same – or a shifting number of other – women friends continued to visit him: his staff called them 'the harem'. The consequences could be tempestuous. Getty, whose evenings were spent in a small room watching television, affected not to hear. He may even have enjoyed the cat fights, of which he was the cause. Although Getty's relations with the world's media could only be described as bleak, the press never drew attention to his voracious sexual appetite, perhaps because it did not fit the image that they had shaped for him as a joyless skinflint.

Getty lived in a Tudor house; his mores had an obvious parallel with those of the Tudor court. But this complex man, dryly dedicated to figures, but also a prey to superstition, irrational fears and hypochondria, personally believed in another historical connection. The remarkable decision to build the Getty Museum in the form of the Villa dei Papyri at Herculaneum appears to have been influenced by the belief that he was a reincarnation of the Emperor Hadrian. Only when his end was near did he – or his immediate entourage – cut himself off from the world, although even then he was not entirely alone. In the spring of 1976, a succession of healers, quacks and alternative therapists were summoned to complement the efforts of his doctor to prolong his life, to the sounds of women screaming for admittance to the bedside of the dying man. 'He was an eccentric and a genius in his way,' observed Pen, 'but very naughty'.[5]

ABOVE Sutton Place was built by the Tudor Sir Richard Weston, a courtier of Henry VIII, who acquired the estate after being one of the jury that convicted the 3rd Duke of Buckingham, its previous owner, of treason.

There is no truth to the rumour that Getty's personal guests at Sutton Place were required to use a public telephone box when making calls. A telephone box was installed, but only for the use of builders, journalists and other people who passed through, who felt entitled to run up the richest man in the world's phone bills.

SIR PAUL GETTY

AT

WORMSLEY PARK

n 1986, John Paul Getty's son, Eugene Paul, although American, was made an honorary Knight of the British Empire as Sir Paul Getty (he did not like the name Eugene). You don't have to look far to discover why he was so honoured. His *Who's Who* entry listed his occupation as 'philanthropist'. His many benefactions fell like a refreshing shower on the parched and sometimes wilting landscape of British culture in the last decades of the twentieth century. The fortunes of the National Gallery and the British Film Institute, in particular, were transformed. The former, ironically perhaps, was given the fighting fund it needed to oppose the might of the Getty Museum in California – the creation, as we have seen, of Sir Paul's father. But his largesse also helped many smaller and more quixotic causes, from Lord's Cricket Ground to cathedrals and churches, from the steamship SS *Great Britain* to a home for retired actors. Regarded, like his father, as a recluse, he broke out of his self-imposed shell towards the end of his life, entertaining friends and neighbours, and gathering his family about him. Wormsley Park in Buckinghamshire was both the setting and the symbol of the golden end of his life's journey. He had travelled a stony road.

PREVIOUS PAGES Wormsley Park, showing the red-brick, eighteenth-century house with the castle-style library hiding in trees to the right. At the top of the photograph is the cricket pitch.

Sir Paul Getty (1932-2003), the bibliophile philanthropist who, by the end of his life, had transformed himself into a quintessential Englishman. In Getty's *Guardian* obituary, the journalist and cricket editor Matthew Engel wrote: 'He would have been a kindly man, even in normal circumstances. But he never knew normality, which is perhaps why he craved it so much.'

RIGHT The Mound stand at Lord's Cricket Ground in London made possible by Sir Paul Getty's generosity.

OPPOSITE Built of knapped flint, Nicholas Johnston's library was designed to enhance the romance of Wormsley, by suggesting an old castle, without overshadowing the main block.

No son or daughter of J. Paul Getty was likely to have enjoyed a warm and stable childhood. Sir Paul's mother, Ann, daughter of Sam Rork, a Hollywood producer, had been the fourth wife; the marriage was not a long one. A point of stability in the young Paul's life was provided by his Roman Catholic education at a Jesuit school, which gave him the anchor of faith in an often tempestuous existence. In the *Oxford Dictionary of National Biography*, the antiques dealer Christopher Gibbs, who knew Getty well, writes of his wild adventures as an undergraduate at San Francisco State University. His military service was spent in Korea, which introduced him to 'the pleasures of the Orient'.

Afterwards, Paul entered the family oil business, first as a petrol pump attendant on a garage forecourt, but soon as the head of Getty Oil Italia. Rome entranced him. It

was the era of la dolce vita, which proved too seductive for his marriage to Gail Harris, daughter of a San Francisco judge, to endure beyond 1964, when they divorced. Their two sons and two daughters saw little of their father. Getty then married Talitha Pol, a beautiful Dutch woman who was the step-granddaughter of the artist Augustus John. Drink and drugs made the 1960s, for Getty, something of a blur. The years were passed in Chelsea and Marrakech, in the company of a 'a diverse group of friends, from Mick Jagger to Gore Vidal, picnicking by mountain streams, supping with Moorish grandees, but equally amused by snake charmers and scallywags from the Djem al-Fna'.[1] Talitha died of a heroin overdose in 1971. Paul retreated to London and the gentle world of bibliophilia. Old books became a passion.

Afterwards, Paul entered the family oil business, first as a petrol pump attendant on a garage forecourt, but soon as the head of Getty Oil Italia.

The equilibrium that Getty was building for himself was overturned when, in 1973, his son, the long-haired, party-loving John Paul III, then aged sixteen, was kidnapped by the Mafia in Rome. They sent a ransom note demanding £17 million for the boy's return. It was initially regarded as a hoax. A second note was delayed by three weeks by a postal strike. Paul Getty asked his father for the money but was refused. Then eighty, J. Paul Getty explained his attitude to paying ransom money in a statement to the press: 'I have 14 grandchildren, and if I pay a penny of ransom, I'll have 14 kidnapped grandchildren.' The Mafia responded by posting the boy's severed ear, making it clear that the rest of him would be returned in small pieces if the ransom was not forthcoming. John Paul III was eventually released, in a malnourished condition, after the payment of a sum, said to be $3 million. By 1981 he had become a junkie, supplementing heroin and cocaine with a daily bottle of bourbon;

that year he suffered liver failure caused by the combination of illicit drugs and others he was taking to kick the habit. He went into a six-week coma, from which he emerged a quadriplegic. Gail took Paul Getty to court in Los Angeles over hospital bills. Chaos seemed to have become manifest. He took refuge in his books.

After the death of J. Paul Getty, Getty fils was a billionaire. His book collecting was given free rein. In the tribute published by *The Bookman* after Paul Getty's death in 2003, Nicholas Barker described the library as 'to be measured by comparison with the great collections of the past – as great as any made in the last century'. When the Pierpont Morgan Library showed an exhibition of its finest glories in 1999, Getty, 'reluctantly, after some bullying', wrote an introduction to the catalogue, describing his first encounters with the *recherché* world of rare book dealers. As a teenager, he had come upon the works of F. Scott Fitzgerald. Some titles had very few copies in print. 'This led me to discover the miracle of the second-hand bookshop and the mystique of the first edition.' Christopher Gibbs wondered – not, surely, very seriously – whether the seed of his book lust had not been sown even earlier, for his father, J. Paul Getty, had

collected books, too: all the glories of British derring-do through history, the complete works of G. A. Henty in their rainbow of gilded publisher's bindings. Did he read these rousing tales to his children? How else did his young son Paul become infected with Britain's island spell?

RIGHT Thatched pavilion and Chiltern woods: the cricket ground at Wormsley, which Sir Paul Getty created, is one of the most beautiful in Britain.

LEFT Here Sir Paul Getty refreshes himself, while talking to the Leicestershire fast bowler Jonathan Agnew; the latter would become familiar to radio's cricketing listenership as 'Aggers'.

BELOW Village cricket match at Wormsley. Getty's love of cricket shows how perilously close he came to crossing the species barrier from red-blooded American to whites-wearing Englishman, although his admiration for the game remained platonic: he never played.

The idea that J. Paul Getty was a hands-on father is, however, fanciful in the extreme.

After military service, Getty went back to 'the enchanting shelves of the used-book dealers in San Francisco at that time', buying one 'of my greatest treasures, and at the same time greatest bargains, the Blake Songs of Innocence and Experience'. His collecting lapsed during the Rome years. It was rekindled in London where he became particularly devoted to the antiquarian booksellers Maggs Brothers of Berkeley Square. Bryan Maggs was 'phenomenally well-versed' in bibliopegy, or the 'great British craft' of bookbinding.[2] Visual appeal was, for Getty, an important criterion when considering a purchase: he liked gorgeous bindings, whether rococo or neoclassical, Jazz Age or 1960s, as well as the beauty of illuminated manuscripts. Rarity and historical association were other factors; Getty collected with discipline. 'The library, therefore,' observed Gibbs in the Pierpont Morgan catalogue, 'has a coherence and an individuality beyond the tedious gathering of a rich man's baubles.' Some of the volumes cost millions of pounds. So big was the collection that Getty decided to erect a purpose-built library to house it. This he did in the shape of a miniature fort designed by Nicholas Johnston. In banded flint, it was attached to the back of Wormsley Park, the country house in Buckinghamshire that he bought in 1984. The photograph accompanying the catalogue portrays him, leathery, hunched and sandal-wearing, in the act of studying an ancient manuscript, against a background of serried shelves and leather bindings. Only a ring on the fourth finger of his right hand hints at a previously more colourful life.

Wormsley became an Elysium. First taken there by Christopher Gibbs, Getty was entranced. He immediately set about putting the estate, which had become run down, into the best possible order. Writing in *Country Life* in 1991, Duff Hart-Davis described how 'Millions have been spent. The point, however, is that everything has been done with exceptional imagination, sympathy and style.'[3] A 4-acre lake was created – not an easy achievement in the bone-dry Chilterns, and only possible after sinking a bore hole several hundred feet deep. A deer park was stocked with red and fallow deer. Eight miles of private road were remade, entered through a set of splendid gates brought from Ireland. Sarsen stones – those mysterious outcrops that heave themselves out of chalk landscapes – were hauled from the Wiltshire Downs and used to make a bridge, some of the library's footings and markers for roads and paths. Woods of ash, beech, wild cherry and oak were planted.

In 1994, Getty married his third wife, Victoria Holdsworth. From the secure base of his new marriage and idyllic country estate, Getty felt able to venture tentatively into the world. He formalised his Anglophilia by adopting British nationality in 1998. He had already made what might be regarded as a symbolic declaration of intent by laying out a cricket pitch, overlooked by a thatched pavilion; he had been introduced to cricket by Mick Jagger. In this ideal setting, surrounded by Chilterns beechwoods, the national game – whichever teams are playing – aspires to the aesthetic status of ballet.

Wormsley Park is now the home of Sir Paul's son, Mark, and every summer the Garsington Opera Festival is held in its grounds.

LEFT The library at Wormsley, designed by Nicholas Johnston, combined the qualities of a library in a college and a great hall.

NOTES

INTRODUCTION

1 Richard W. Davis, '"We Are All Americans Now!" Anglo-American Marriages in the Later Nineteenth Century', *Proceedings of the American Philosophical Society*, vol. 135, no. 2 (June 1991), pp.140–99.

2 Ruth Brandon, *The Dollar Princesses*, 1980, p. 31.

3 Davis. op. cit., p. 145.

4 See Clive Aslet, *The American Country House*, 1990, p. 21.

5 Ibid. p. 25. Kimball appears to be quoting Benjamin Howitt, *The Rural Life of England*, vol. i, 1838, p. 27.

6 Constance Cary Harrison, *Fads and Fancies of Representative Americans at the Beginning of the Twentieth Century*, 1905.

7 Ronald Tree's son Michael lived at Mereworth Castle in Kent in the 1950s and 1960s.

8 In *Daisy Miller*, that charm worried Count Otto who, surprisingly for a Henry James character, strikes an almost Wodehousean note:

He could immediately think of a dozen men he knew who had married American girls. There appeared now to be a constant danger of marrying the American girl: it was something one had to reckon with, like the railway, the telegraph, the discovery of dynamite, the Chassepot rifle, the Socialistic spirit: it was one of the complications of modern life.

British mothers with daughters to marry bemoaned what seemed like unfair competition. The Prince of Wales, however, was a fan.

9 S. Hignett, *Brett: From Bloomsbury to New Mexico. A Biography*, 1984. Even so, there were limits, and Harcourt crossed them when making overtures to the twelve-year-old Edward James. His mother, Mrs Willie James, took the matter up, but Harcourt died: whether intentionally or not, he had taken an overdose of a sleeping draught. He was found dead in his bedroom at 69 Brook Street.

10 His mistress, Elinor Glyn, read about the engagement in the newspaper while staying with Curzon; he was – except for his devotion to Mary – a cold fish.

FLORA SHARON AT EASTON NESTON

1 James Miller, 'Easton Neston: a History,' essay in Sotheby's sale catalogue, 2005, p. 24.

2 Michael J. Makley, *The Infamous King of the Comstock: William Sharon and the Gilded Age in the West.*

3 Quoted Makley, op. cit., p.137.

4 Makley, op. cit., p. 156.

5 Miller, op. cit., p. 93.

6 According to James Miller, op. cit., p. 27.

WALTER BURNS AT BROOK STREET AND NORTH MYMMS

1 Biographical details from obituary in *Harvard College Class of 1856, Secretary's Report*, 1899, p. 15.

2 Clive Aslet, 'Billiards on Sundays', *Country Life*, 12 November 1981, p. 162.

THE ASTORS AT CLIVEDEN AND HEVER CASTLE

1 William Bray and John Forster (eds), *The Diary and Correspondence of John Evelyn, F.R.S.*, 1870, vol. 2, p. 141.

2 For the early history of Cliveden, see James Crathorne, *Cliveden: The Place and the People*, London, 1995; Jonathan Marsden, *Cliveden, Buckinghamshire*, 1994.

3 Michael Astor, *Tribal Feeling*, 1963, pp.17–18.

4 Philip Tilden, *True Remembrance*, 1954, p. 114.

5 Norman Rose, *The Cliveden Set*, London, 2000, p. 32.

6 Christopher Sykes, *Nancy: The Life of Lady Astor*, 1972, p. 92.

WILLIE JAMES AT WEST DEAN

1 Robert Glass Cleland, *A History of Phelps Dodge*, New York: Alfred A. Knopf, 1952; Phyllis B. Dodge, *Tales of the Phelps Dodge Family*, New York: New York Historical Society (June 1987); Richard Lowitt, *A Merchant Prince of the Nineteenth Century*, New York: Columbia University Press, 1954.

2 Thomas Seccombe, rev. Elizabeth Baigent, 'James, Frank Linsly', *Oxford Dictionary of National Biography*, www.oxforddnb.com.

CONSUELO VANDERBILT AT BLENHEIM PALACE

1 Quoted in John Hardy, 'Blenheim and the Louis XIV Revival', *Country Life*, 30 January 1975.

2 Charles Jennings, *Them and Us*, Stroud, 2007, pp.199–200.

3 Consuelo Vanderbilt Balsan, *The Glitter and the Gold*, 1952.

ANDREW CARNEGIE AT SKIBO CASTLE

1 Joseph Frazier Wall, *Skibo*, 2002, p. 40.

2 Andrew Carnegie, *Autobiography of Andrew Carnegie*, 1920, p. 217.

3 Wall, op. cit., p. 47.

4 T. H. S. Escott, *Edward VII and his Court*.

5 Janet Waymark, *Thomas Mawson: Life, Gardens and Landscapes*, London, 2009, p. 60.

MAY GOELET AT FLOORS CASTLE

1 Anita Leslie, *Edwardians in Love*, 1974, p. 311.

2 Ruth Brandon, *The Dollar Princesses*, 1980, pp. 70–71; quoted in Cornelius Vanderbilt Jr, *Queen of the Golden Age*, pp.187–8.

3 Consuelo Vanderbilt Balsan, *The Glitter and the Gold*, 1952.

4 Henry H. Klein, *Dynastic America and Those Who Own It*, 1921, p. 37.

5 Obituary, 'Dowager Duchess of Roxburghe', *The Times*, 27 April, 1937, p. 18.

6 http://thehistorybox.com/ny_city/society/articles/nycity_society_obit_goelet_1897_article00268.htm

7 *The Times*, 30 September 1932.

8 Marcus Binney, 'Floors Castle, Roxburghshire', *Country Life*, 11 and 18 May 1978.

WILFRED AND BERTHA BUCKLEY AT MOUNDSMERE MANOR

1 *The Times*, 27 April 1937; appreciation (after obit) by R.L. of F.

LAWRENCE JOHNSTON AT HIDCOTE MANOR

1 Alvilda Lees-Milne, 'Lawrence Johnston, Creator of Hidcote Garden', *Hortus Revisited: a Twenty-First Birthday Anthology*, 2008, pp. 36–44.

2 V. Sackville-West, 'Hidcote Manor garden', *RHS Journal*, 74/2 (1949), p. 476.

MAUD CUNARD AT NEVILL HOLT

1 Daphne Fielding, *Emerald and Nancy*, 1968, p. 2.

2 Lois G. Gordon, *Nancy Cunard: Heiress, Muse, Political Idealist*, p. 11.

3 Cecil Beaton, *The Book of Beauty*. Quoted in Daphne Fielding, *Emerald and Nancy*, 1968, p. 24

4 Harold, Acton, *Memoirs of an Aesthete*.

5 *TES*, 11 May 2008.

GORDON SELFRIDGE AND HENGISTBURY HEAD

1 A. H. Williams, *No Name on the Door*, 1956, p. 156.

2 Ibid.

3 Philip Tilden, *True Remembrances*, 1954, pp. 52–3.

NANCY LANCASTER AT KELMARSH HALL, DITCHLEY PARK AND HASELEY COURT

1 Peter Pennoyer and Anne Walker, *The Architecture of Delano and Aldrich*, New York, 2003.

2 Quoted in James Fox, *Five Sisters: The Langhornes of Virginia*, New York, 2000, p. 213.

3 Robert Becker, *Nancy Lancaster: Her Life, Her World, Her Art*, New York, 1996, p.174.

4 Ibid., p. 203.

5 Ibid., p. 207.

WILLIAM RANDOLPH HEARST AT ST DONAT'S

1 Ben Procter, *William Randolph Hearst: The Later Years 1911–1951*, p. 148.

2 David Nasaw, *The Chief: The Life of William Randolph Hearst*, pp. 233–4

3 Royal Commission on Ancient and Historical Monuments in Wales, *An Inventory of the Ancient Monuments in Glamorgan*, vol. 3.

LADY BAILLIE AT LEEDS CASTLE

1 *The Times*, 12 September 1974.

2 Leeds Castle guidebook, p. 20. For Leeds Castle see also Alan Bignell, *Lady Baillie at Leeds Castle*, n.d.

3 Alice Wykeham-Martin Pollock, *Portrait of My Victorian Youth*, 1971, p. 61.

4 Ibid.

5 Curtis Harnack, *Gentlemen on the Prairie: Victorians in Pioneer Iowa*, pp. 108–9.

6 David Niven, *The Moon's a Balloon*, 1971, p. 209.

7 Sally Beddell Smith, *Reflected Glory: The Life of Pamela Churchill Harriman*, 1996, p. 49.

8 Ibid., p. 50. Quote from Susan Remington-Hobbs.

9 John Cornforth, 'Boudin at Leeds Castle I and II', *Country Life*, 14 and 21 April 1983.

THE PRINCE OF WALES AND WALLIS SIMPSON AT FORT BELVEDERE

1 The Duke of Windsor, *A King's Story*, 1951, p. 237.

2 Charles Jennings, *Them and Us*, Stroud, 2007, p. 208.

3 Ibid., p. 211.

4 Ibid., p. 216.

5 Christopher Hussey, 'Fort Belvedere Surrey I and II', *Country Life*, 19 and 26 November 1959.

6 Philip Ziegler, *King Edward VIII*, 1990, p. 232.

7 Michael Bloch quoted in ibid., p. 280.

8 The Duke of Windsor, op. cit. p. 405.

'CHIPS' CHANNON AT 5 BELGRAVE SQUARE AND KELVEDON HALL

1 Robert Rhodes James (ed.), *'Chips': The Diaries of Sir Henry Channon*, 1967, p. 38.

2 Quoted in Richard Davenport-Hines, 'Channon, Sir Henry [Chips]', *Oxford Dictionary of National Biography*, www.oxforddnb.com.

3 Robert Rhodes James (ed), *'Chips': The Diaries of Sir Henry Channon*, 1967, p. 10.

4 Ibid., p. 9.

5 Christopher Hussey, '5, Belgrave Square, London', *Country Life*, 26 February 1938, p. 222.

6 Christopher Hussey, 'Kelvedon Hall I and II', *Country Life*, 3 and 10 May 1941.

J. PAUL GETTY AT SUTTON PLACE

1 J. Paul Getty, *As I See It*, 1976, p. 317.

2 M. Goronwy Rees, *The Multi-Millionaires*, 1961, p. 16.

3 Getty, op. cit., pp. 227–8.

4 Russell Miller, *The House of Getty*, 1985.

5 Ibid., p. 302.

SIR PAUL GETTY AT WORMSLEY PARK

1 Christopher Gibbs, 'Getty, Sir (John) Paul', *Oxford Dictionary of Natial Biography*, www.oxforddnb.com.

2 The Wormsley Library, *A Personal Selection by Sir Paul Getty, KBE*, 2007.

3 Duff Hart-Davis, 'Waking the White Ghost', *Country Life*, 5 April 1991, p. 82.

INDEX

Page numbers in *italic* refer to illustrations